OTHER BOOKS BY ANNE WICKLUND

My Ears Have a Wet Nose: Acquiring, Training and Loving a Hearing Dog

I Have a Wet Nose … and I Have a Job

Handbook for Service Dogs

Truths and Myths about Working Dogs

Handbook for Service Dogs

Truths and Myths about Working Dogs

By

Anne & Wayne Wicklund

MrPAWS by Snow

Fountain Hills, Arizona

Published by MrPAWS by Snow
PO Box 17954
Fountain Hills AZ 85269
www.handbookforservicedogs.com

ISBN 978-0-578-16329-1
ISBN 10-0-578-16329-2
Printed in the United States of America
1 2 3 4 5   19 18 17 16 15

Library of Congress Cataloging-in-Publication Data
Wicklund, Anne and Wicklund, Wayne
Handbook for Service Dogs

Library of Congress Control Number: 2015910582
MrPAWS by Snow, Fountain Hills, AZ

Part IV contains an excerpt from *The Golden Bridge*, ed. Patty Dobbs Gross (2005): 199-204, reprinted with the author's permission.

Front cover photograph by Sara Goodnick
Back cover photographs by Susan Hafty

This publication is designed to provide accurate and authoritative information with regard to the subject matter covered. It is sold with the understanding that the publisher is not engaged in rendering legal, accounting, or other professional advice. If legal advice or other expert assistance is required, the services of a competent professional person should be sought.
—From a *Declaration of Principles* jointly adopted by a Committee of the American Bar Association and a Committee of Publishers and Associations

Many of the designations used by manufacturers and sellers to distinguish their products are claimed as trademarks. Where such designations appear in this book and the publisher was aware of a trademark claim, the designations have been printed with initial capital letters.

Available from Amazon.com and other retail and online outlets

For Snow Prince

Contents

Acknowledgments

We'd like to give special thanks to a few people for their help and support. In terms of publishing and production, we thank CreateSpace, a division of Amazon.com, Inc., and Senior Publishing Consultant Gaines Hill.

Our heartfelt thanks go to our friends at TOP DOG, to Stacey Larsen at Puppy Prep School, to the Facebook community of people with service dogs, and to our fabulous customers, who inspire us every day. Without them all—and their questions and suggestions—we would never have known what you needed to know.

We are particularly indebted to Debbie Skehen for her generosity and her ongoing encouragement of our work and to Joanne Thyken for reading and commenting on sections of the manuscript.

Our grateful appreciation to Mary Ann M. Bosnos, our editor, for her unfailing good nature and attention to countless details.

Introduction

Why is it so hard to get basic truths about service dogs? Because the law is vague. Because many of the people or organizations who give you the answers have agendas of their own. Because much of the available information is inaccurate.

People who are coping with disability often become discouraged or overwhelmed when they can't find clear information on whether or how service dogs might help them. Those who have already partnered with service dogs sometimes lack essential information.

We aim to give honest and complete answers to most of their questions—with humor and also with the realization that this is a very serious subject.

Our service dog, Snow Prince, saved Wayne's life every day in many different ways. He came to us as a pet, became a hearing-assist dog, and then added medical assistance to his repertoire. His versatility was amazing. Snow Prince went to conventions, flew on airplanes, took cruises, and rode shuttle buses and tour buses. This type of lifestyle is extremely stressful to animals, but service dogs must be able to maintain their composure throughout such events. They must be sociable, flexible, and unflappable.

Wayne and Snow Prince were so deeply bonded that, when they talked to each other, strangers marveled at the love, trust, and respect that these two shared. When Snow Prince passed away Wayne was in terrible distress. He tried to do without a dog, but after a couple of months he realized that this was not an option because of his disabilities. We sought and found Snow Shadow, a.k.a. Shadow. He is very different from Snow Prince in size, temperament, and character but is just as dedicated to Wayne's well being.

How does Wayne rely on Snow Shadow?

❖ His dog hears for him. Shadow lets Wayne know if

people are nearby or are trying to get his attention. If Anne and Wayne are together in public and she turns a corner, Wayne instantly becomes confused and nervous because he does not know where she is—he is upset because he can't hear her. When this happens, Shadow leads Wayne to Anne.

❖ Snow Shadow helps Wayne with mobility. He braces Wayne, pulls him, and assists him to stand or sit. Since Wayne suffered a traumatic brain injury he has developed major-motor-skill problems. Sometimes he can't think clearly or speak. When this happens, the dog leads Wayne to safety or summons help.

❖ Wayne experiences seizures due to post-traumatic stress disorder (PTSD). When he has a seizure, Shadow lies across his lap to calm him until the episode passes.

❖ Wayne's dog does not leave his side, but will attract attention or assistance when needed. Knowing that Snow Shadow is always there to help him gives Wayne confidence, relieves his anxiety, and allows him to enjoy the normal activities of daily living.

Having a service dog can also be inconvenient—that is something to think about. What are some of the challenges for people with service dogs?

❖ Riding on public transportation—when your dog is sitting in a set of seats with you while your spouse or partner must sit alone in another seat.

❖ Having to use a regular stall in public bathrooms instead of a handicapped stall.

❖ Staying in a hotel and having to go down to the street to find someplace for your dog to relieve himself. This can be particularly difficult at night.

❖ Having to rely on an emergency friend to care for your service dog if you must go into the hospital, have an accident, or are otherwise incapacitated.

❖ Putting on and taking off the dog's raincoat and wiping

him down with a small towel after he has been in the rain.

❖ Drying the dog's feet and legs each time he is out in the snow.

❖ Putting on and taking off the dog's boots for walking on hot ground or pavement.

❖ Finding a place for your dog to relieve himself if you are living in a condo or apartment with no yard.

❖ Dealing with restaurants that really don't want you there, but know they have to let you in.

❖ Finding somewhere for your dog to relieve himself at a convention center, museum, concert hall, place of worship, movie theater, sports arena, or other public place. This can be especially difficult in downtown areas.

❖ Finding a place where your dog can relieve himself at an airport. Airports are now required to have relief areas outside; these are usually near the baggage-claim area. But many still do not have relief areas for dogs within secure perimeters.

For all of these reasons and more, you must carefully consider whether having a service dog would actually be a help and what breed would best fit your circumstances. You must consider cost, size, grooming needs, and other factors that will make having a service dog a pleasant and satisfying experience versus a chore.

> This book does not cover service dogs for the blind or visually impaired because our experience is primarily with hearing-assist, medical-assist, and mobility-assist dogs. There are many resources containing a wealth of information on service dogs for the blind, and we refer the reader to those.

PART I

What Is a Service Dog?

What exactly is a service dog? People who depend on them use various terms: working dog, assistance dog, comfort companion, or therapy dog. The Americans with Disabilities Act of 1990 (ADA)

defines a service dog as any dog that is individually trained to perform tasks for the benefit of an individual with a disability, including a physical, psychiatric, intellectual, or other disability. By law, a service dog is not considered a pet, may be any breed or size, and is not legally required to wear tags or special equipment. It is prohibited by law to require proof or "certification" of a service dog's training. Service dogs perform mobility, hearing, guide, seizure-alert, emotional-support, and other work needed by a disabled person.

Service dogs are expected to perform specific tasks, for which they have been trained, for specific individuals with whom they partner. These tasks may include but are not limited to:

- Alerting individuals who are deaf or hard of hearing
- Providing protection or rescue assistance
- Guiding blind or visually impaired individuals
- Pulling a wheelchair
- Fetching items
- Alerting their partners to impending seizures
- Opening doors
- Picking up items
- Sniffing out allergens
- Calming an anxiety or panic attack

More specifically, the ADA defines service dogs as "dogs that are individually trained to do work or perform tasks for people with disabilities. Examples of such work or tasks include guiding people who are blind, alerting people who are deaf, pulling a wheelchair, alerting and protecting a person who is having a seizure, reminding a person with mental illness to take prescribed medications, calming a person with Post Traumatic Stress Disorder (PTSD) during an anxiety attack, or performing other duties."

Before a 2010 revision of ADA regulations limited approved service animals to dogs and miniature horses, some people used cats or monkeys. Mini-horses are still used, but dogs remain by far the most popular service animals.

The term "service-dog team" is used to describe the combination of a service dog that has been trained to meet specific disability-related needs and the handler/partner whom that particular dog assists. A service dog trains for up to two or more years and can perform a wide variety of tasks tailored to his partner's needs. Often people who rely on service dogs have multiple disabilities and needs.

Service-Dog Tasks

Per the ADA, a service animal must perform specific functions for his handler—any functions necessitated by the disability. Here are some of the ways in which service dogs help their partners:

Alerting: A service dog alerts on a number of different issues in order to ensure his partner's safety and well being. He may alert by nudging, twirling, tugging, pulling, sitting and staring, or lying on a part of his partner's body—for example, lying on the chest to protect his partner from harm during a seizure. Service dogs should never nip or bite when alerting.

Providing Emotional Support: People who are grieving or are receiving medical care for emotional issues may benefit from an emotional-support dog. People with PTSD or brain-chemistry malfunctions also benefit.

While a dog's companionship may provide emotional support, comfort, or a sense of security, this in and of itself does NOT qualify as a "trained task" under the ADA, and thus it does not confer the legal right to take that dog out in public as a legitimate service dog. Setting up a realistic training plan to transform a suitable dog into an obedient, task-trained service dog is the only way to legally qualify that dog to become a service dog whose disabled handler is legally permitted to take him into restaurants, grocery stores, hospitals, medical offices, and other public places. We recommend reading the International Association of Assistance Dog Partners (IAADP) "Minimum Training Standards for Public Access" for further guidance at www.iaadp.org.

Emotional-support dogs perform tasks such as these:

- Bringing medication
- Bringing a beverage so the partner can take medication
- Bringing the emergency phone during a crisis
- Answering the doorbell
- Calling 911 on a rescue phone
- Bringing help indoors
- Providing speech-impairment assistance
- Assisting the partner to rise and steady her/himself
- Arousing from fear paralysis or a dissociative spell

Aiding with Mobility: Mobility-assist dogs help with mobility and balance. They are usually (but not always) large dogs that can brace a partner or pull him/her into standing position.

Medical Alerting: Medical-assist dogs can detect a partner's impending seizure or asthma attack. Usually the dog can anticipate such events around fifteen minutes in advance, allowing his partner time to sit, lie down, or stop driving.

People who have been house bound for years for fear of experiencing a seizure or other medical event in public have found that, with the help of medical-assist dogs, they can again enjoy full, active lives.

Detecting Scents/Allergens: Service dogs with partners who suffer from allergies or lung disorders are trained to lead their partners away from allergic triggers. Wayne's dog will not allow him to be near cats (Wayne is highly allergic) or in a place where scents such as cleaning chemicals might affect his lungs.

Guiding or Herding: Service dogs not only do guide work for the blind or visually impaired but also partner with autism and Alzheimer's patients. They "herd" their partners and keep them safe by preventing them from hurting themselves or wandering into danger.

Which Breeds Can Be Service Dogs?

It is a common misconception that a small or tiny-breed dog cannot function as a service dog. Any service dog's job must be broken down into tasks that the dog can perform. Tasks are layered with consecutive cues given to complete each task. Small service dogs can easily meet the challenges put to them.

Not all disabilities require assistance with tasks involving heavy doors or a person's dead weight. The service dog may be needed only for tasks that can easily be performed by a small dog such as retrieving objects, sound alerting, or seizure alerting.

A small dog may often be the best option, especially in cities, where people tend to live in small apartments rather than in large homes. And many disabled seniors prefer small-breed service dogs because travel by car, cab, or plane is easier, the quantity of food consumed is considerably less, and the dog requires less living space than a large dog would need.

It is unfortunate that many small-service-dog handlers avoid the spotlight for fear of rejection or altercations. They lose not only the full benefit of partnering with a service dog but also an opportunity to educate the public.

Recent media coverage of "fake," poorly trained, or insufficiently trained service dogs has heightened difficulties for the small-service-dog handler, who must perform twice as well to gain public acceptance and admission into public places and on public transit.

People are accustomed to seeing large-breed service dogs, but a small-breed dog is almost immediately thought of as a charlatan. Even service-dog training programs can sometimes overlook the abilities of small-breed working dogs. The Golden Retrievers, Labs, Great Danes, and Shepherds tend to claim center stage. They are known for their even temperaments and their strength for pulling wheelchairs, opening heavy doors, bracing, or helping a partner to get up or down. But the small breeds are perfect partners for many disabled people.

How Does a Service Dog Alert?

What does a service dog alert to? And how does he alert? The method used is specific to his partner's particular needs. There should never be tugging, tearing, biting, or nipping. Some ways in which service dogs alert include:

- Nudging/nuzzling—the dog gently nudges his partner's hand or knee with his nose.
- Touching—the dog touches where he wants his partner to look or touches the object that he wants his partner to notice.

- ❖ Leaning—the dog leans into his partner to protect.
- ❖ Pawing—the dog gently paws his partner's arm or knee to let him/her know that something is amiss and needs attention; if his partner does not respond, the dog repeats the alert in a firmer manner.
- ❖ Pushing—the dog pushes or herds his partner either into the place he wants his partner to notice or out of the place that represents a danger.
- ❖ Hitting—if his partner doesn't pay attention, the dog gently hits him/her with his paws to attract attention.
- ❖ Twirling—some dogs (especially small dogs) actually twirl in little circles to get a partner's attention.
- ❖ Turning his head and looking in the direction of the object of attention.
- ❖ Stopping—the dog will not move forward.
- ❖ Pulling—the dog pulls his partner by the wrist or pulls on the leash to remove his partner from danger.
- ❖ Looking toward sound to draw attention in that direction.

How a service dog alerts is influenced by what his partner's particular needs are, who trained the dog, and where the dog was trained. Most agencies have created standardized approaches to training. This is necessary because they are training service dogs *en masse* so that the dogs can be used by unknown persons who go through their selection process.

Wayne's dog began to alert spontaneously on Wayne's growing mobility issues and on Wayne's allergy to cats (the dog detects the dander on cat owners' clothes and in their cars).

7

The bottom line is this: If your service dog is acting strangely, he is communicating with you. *PAY ATTENTION* and *LISTEN* to your dog. He knows what he is doing. There is no right or wrong way for him to alert as long as it suits you and is not disruptive to people around you.

If your dog is repeating a behavior that you do not understand, take a step back and analyze what, when, where, and why. You will figure out what the dog is telling you. Sometimes it is as simple as the fact that the dog knows you need to stop and rest. Dogs are not stubborn "just because."

What Does a Medical-Assist Dog Do?

A medical-assist dog helps with a medical disability, e.g., spinal injury, hearing impairment, seizure disorder, diabetes, mobility issues, etc. His ability to detect changes in bodily odors or body rhythms allows him to alert on various issues.

Dogs are amazingly sensitive to body rhythms and odors. Once you've established a bond with your dog, you will notice that he communicates information about your physical or emotional condition. Learn to listen to your dog. Pay attention when he exhibits a behavior consistently—he is letting you know, for example, that:

> ➤ You are tired and should lie down. (Snow Prince and Shadow have both refused to move forward, even on a "walk," if they sensed that Wayne was tired.)

> ➤ You are about to have a seizure. Some dogs twirl or lie across your body to alert, giving you time to lie down and not hurt yourself.
> ➤ You need to eat. (Shadow nudges Anne's hand and herds her into the kitchen if she needs to eat—she is diabetic.)
> ➤ You need to stop working. (Shadow, who weighs more than ninety pounds, crawls into Wayne's lap and won't let him continue working if he senses that Wayne needs to rest.)

Dogs can multitask. Wayne has multiple medical conditions, and Shadow adjusts as necessary. When he sees that Wayne needs to know something, he will find a way to tell him. Shadow started out as a hearing-assist dog, then became an allergy-alert dog, then added mobility assistance, etc.

What Does a Hearing-Assist Dog Do?

A hearing-assist dog will alert on a variety of sounds and dangers. This allows you to be aware of your surroundings and take proper precautions. For example:

- ❧ Inside the home, the dog will alert if water is boiling on the stove, a kettle whistling, baby crying, doorbell ringing, someone yelling, water running, telephone ringing, someone calling your name.
- ❧ Outside the home, the dog will alert to traffic dangers, persons around you when walking, wildlife living in your area or where you are visiting, and other animals.

Shadow recently alerted Wayne to a rattlesnake—which Wayne did not see and could not hear—on our back patio by jumping in front of Wayne and pushing him out of harm's way. Shadow definitely earned his dinner that night and a doggie biscuit to boot!

What Does a Mobility-Assist Dog Do?

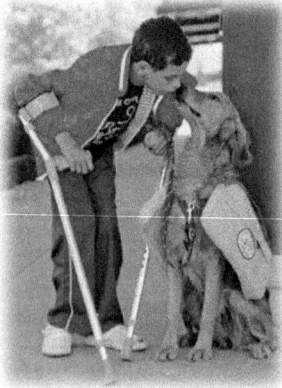

Bracing and pulling are very important types of assistance that mobility-assist dogs provide for their partners. To brace, the dog digs in his feet, stands very still, and allows his partner to pull her/himself up or to maintain his/her balance until ready to move forward. Once the person is stabilized, the dog proceeds as needed. By pulling, the dog helps his partner to stand or sit, move forward, get to his/her car, or whatever motion is required. Wayne sometimes loses his balance for no apparent reason; Shadow stabilizes him by bracing and leaning into him. When Wayne is sufficiently recovered, they will move. Sometimes Wayne tells his dog to "take him home" and Shadow pulls him to a safe place. Shadow always knows whether we are in a hotel, on a cruise ship, in a grocery store, or in our hometown.

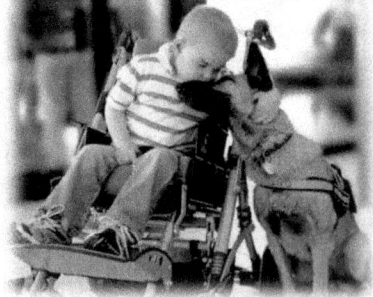

They'll go out of their way to get you up and outside. Even if it means spending all their time pushing a wheelchair

10

People with mobility challenges rely on their dogs to pick up objects, open doors, pull wheelchairs, retrieve, remind them to take medication, bring help, or immobilize them in the event of a seizure. Mobility-assist dogs can be trained to help with the laundry and to retrieve items from the refrigerator.

To assist with laundry, the commands could be:

🐾 look

🐾 get it

🐾 hold

🐾 bring

🐾 give or drop

What Does an Emotional-Support Dog Do?

Emotional-support dogs are a very real and necessary addition to today's society and are recognized as such by ADA guidelines, which state: "Service dogs perform tasks to mitigate certain disabling illnesses classified as mental impairments . . . for panic disorder, PTSD and depression."

These dogs calm their partners and help them to focus. They are especially attuned to people who are recovering from emotional trauma, PTSD, or cancer. And they are effective in helping children and adults with autism.

Emotional-support dogs perform a long list of tasks, including:

🐾 Alerting to an impending anxiety attack

🐾 Leading a partner to a quiet area to prevent an anxiety attack

11

- Reminding a partner to take medication
- Clearing a room to ease a partner's anxiety
- Providing passive blocking to lower anxiety
- Providing deep-pressure therapy to calm a partner
- Creating space between an anxious partner and others, when needed
- Preventing a partner from stepping into traffic or other danger during a dissociative episode
- Getting help when a partner has a stress-related seizure
- Preventing a partner from injuring her/himself from a fall during a seizure
- Rolling a partner during a seizure
- Waking a partner from a seizure
- Preventing a panic attack or stress-related seizure on an airline flight or other public transport

Petting an animal releases a hormone called oxytocin, which has a calming effect on the individual. This can help people with emotional issues to be focused enough to leave their homes, maintain employment, and handle many other challenges.

PTSD affects not only people who have suffered trauma—e.g., an assault, a car accident, a serious illness—but also veterans returning from military service. The U.S. Department of Veterans Affairs (VA) has found that these men and women benefit by interacting with service dogs, which can awaken someone from a nightmare or help a disoriented individual refocus. The VA will help pay for the care of a veteran's service dog, but will not assist in acquiring one. There are organizations that donate dogs to veterans and to other people in need.

Taking care of an animal helps disabled individuals by distracting them from their own disabilities—they must focus on caring for the animal. There are service cats, but as of 2010 they are no longer recognized by the ADA as service animals.

We know a woman who suffers from PTSD and the alphabet soup of problems that come with it. She is a brave person who served in the U.S. Navy for six years. She was raped and left with emotional scars that will haunt her for the rest of her life. She was advised that an emotional-support dog would help her to heal and that she could and should start working with one. She looked at many dogs until she found the one that was a good fit for her. In February 2015 she started living and working with a fourteen-pound mix—this has opened the world to her. She walked into a shopping mall for the first time in 22 years! She ate out for the first time in many years. Her dog knows when she starts to have an attack and cues her to refocus. When she panics, he calms her; when she cries, he comforts her. The changes that emotional-support dogs can make in the lives of their partners border on the miraculous.

An emotional-support dog may also perform a medical-assist function for his owner. It is important to recognize that these ARE service dogs, and they need to be identified as such in order to be allowed access to public places. We recommend that they be identified as medical-assist dogs for privacy reasons—you may not want strangers to know what your disability is.

What Does a Therapy Dog Do?

Therapy dogs give comfort and affection to people in hospitals, nursing homes, mental institutions, schools, and stressful situations such as disaster areas. Funeral homes are increasingly using therapy dogs to comfort mourners.

It is important to note that therapy dogs are NOT service dogs. Service dogs directly assist humans and have a legal right to accompany their handlers. Therapy dogs do not provide direct assistance, do not have legal rights to travel everywhere, and must be invited by institutions. Most institutions have rigorous requirements regarding therapy dogs.

> One woman had been diagnosed with PTSD. Her adopted pet evolved into a service dog. She didn't actually know she needed a service dog until she met this dog. He absolutely knew how to calm her down. He weighed less than five pounds, and anyone who met him felt better just holding him. She did NOT have to train him to do this; he just naturally reacts to her stress in a calming fashion. He is an extremely well behaved, docile dog. He knows very few commands. He doesn't need to; he is almost always in her arms or within arm's reach of her. People need to understand that there are many, many disabilities—not all of which are visible.

A therapy dog's primary job is to allow unfamiliar people to make physical contact with him and to enjoy that contact. Children in particular enjoy hugging animals; adults usually enjoy simply petting the dog. The dog might need to be lifted onto, or climb onto, an invalid's lap or bed and sit or lie comfortably there. Many dogs add to the visiting experience by performing small tricks for their audiences or by playing carefully structured games.

Although they do not have the same legal rights that service dogs have, therapy dogs provide a much-needed service. They have a life-affirming effect that can be vitally important.

Whereas a therapy dog gives comfort to a variety of people, a service dog partners with a specific individual. It is unwise to have a dog do both, since that can confuse the dog about whether or when he is working. If it is imperative that the dog serve both functions, the dog's vest should be removed when he is allowed to be sociable so that he will learn to make the distinction.

Researchers are learning that dogs may provide probiotic benefits by licking. Their saliva may transmit beneficial gut bacteria. Researchers at the University of Arizona and the University of California at San Diego are studying whether living with a dog improves the human microbiome.

Dr. Rob Knight, an internationally known expert on the human microbiome, is leading the UC San Diego portion of the study. He says: "The idea of combining animal, human and environmental health, and seeing the whole picture through the lens of the microbes that we share, is an increasing direction for research." There is a growing amount of evidence, Dr. Knight says, that children in dog-owning families have lower incidence of asthma and allergies.

"Multiple lines of evidence suggest that dog microbiota cause this beneficial effect," said Dr. Charles Raison, the study's principal investigator. "There's epidemiological work showing that kids raised with dogs don't tend to get allergies and asthma," Raison said. "So we think that dogs have anti-inflammatory effects, based on effects in kids, and increasingly we think now that maybe it's because of sharing the microbiota."[1]

Fake Service Dogs

Service dogs are not "pets." They are as important to their partners' day-to-day life, mobility, and ability to function as a wheelchair is to someone with a disability that warrants its use.

The ADA protects disabled individuals' right to be accompanied by their service dogs in public places not normally considered dog friendly.

State and local governments, businesses, and organizations that serve the public generally must allow service animals to accompany their handlers in all areas of a facility where the public is normally allowed to go. For example, in a hospital it would be inappropriate to exclude a service animal from areas such as patient rooms, clinics, cafeterias, or examination rooms. However, it may be appropriate to exclude a service animal from operating rooms or burn

---

[1] Bradley J. Fikes, "Dog germs may be good for you," *The San Diego Union-Tribune*, March 17, 2015, accessed June 16, 2015, http://www.utsandiego.com/news/2015/mar/17/dog-germs-probiotics/

units, where the animal's presence may compromise a sterile environment.

There are, however, some requirements. Service dogs must be leashed, harnessed, or tethered unless such a device would interfere with the dog's ability to perform his work, in which case the dog must be under full control of his handler through voice or hand signals.

Service dogs are well trained to not be disruptive in public. You will never see a trained service dog jumping up at people, barking, growling (unless alerting his partner to a problem), or even relieving himself inappropriately.

Still, despite laws that both define a service animal and explain the rights and requirements of service-dog teams, the general public is largely unaware and misinformed.

Service dogs are NOT legally required to wear vests, collars, or bandanas that specifically identify them as service animals, nor are the dogs or their handlers required to obtain certain licenses, identification cards, or official certification. There is no central governing agency that trains, certifies, or otherwise verifies the legitimacy of a service animal. There is no official training or obedience protocol to which all service dogs must adhere. The only rule is that service dogs cannot "cause a disturbance" while in public.

Although service-dog vests, bandanas, or other forms of identification are not required, a vast majority of legitimate service dogs do wear them in a simple effort by their disabled handlers to go about their day peacefully without disruption or confrontation.

So, what's to prevent a person's fraudulently strapping a service-dog vest onto his/her pet dog and walking through the local mall? Truthfully, not much.

While the federal government has done an excellent job of putting easily enforceable laws into place to establish and protect the rights of disabled persons and their service dogs at a national level, little has been done to prevent the fraudulent misrepresentation of family pets as service dogs. Ambiguity in the definition of a service animal, lack of a central governing and certifying organization, and business owners' fear of both public backlash and costly litigation have allowed tens of thousands of people to misrepresent the family pet as a service animal.

Because of online or fraudulent service-animal "certification" and "registries," there are several pet iguanas that have been "registered" and issued documentation and "ID cards" identifying them as legitimate service animals.

> Monkeys are, in fact, often very valuable aids to people who are unable to use their upper bodies. Before the ADA removed monkeys from the list of approved service animals, they were usually registered by the state and well trained. Monkeys can live for over 20 years.

The laws are so vague that, prior to 2010, when the definition of a service animal was revised to include only dogs and, in some cases, miniature horses, it wasn't unheard of for people to claim a cat, a pet monkey, an alpaca, a turkey, a turtle, even a reptile as a legitimate service animal, thereby granting themselves the authority to take those animals into public places and to avoid paying fees associated with taking animals into hotels, into rental properties, and onboard airplanes or other public transportation. Because businesses and their employees usually don't understand the laws, they see a vest or an ID card (possibly fake) and believe the animal is legit!

Although the ADA's service-dog policies apply on a national level, enforcing those policies falls to the individual states. To date, only sixteen states have laws that prohibit misrepresenting a service dog or misrepresenting oneself as disabled. This leaves local authorities and business owners with their hands tied.

To protect the privacy of the disabled, very limited inquiries into the legitimacy of a service dog are allowed. Businesses, staff, and officials may legally ask only two questions of a service-dog handler:

1. Is the dog a service animal required because of a disability?
2. What work or task has the dog been trained to perform?

It is unlawful to ask about a handler's disability, to request the handler's medical documentation, to ask to see the dog's identification card, to request documentation of the dog's training, or to ask that the dog demonstrate his ability to perform the work or task.

Fixing this severely broken system isn't quite as easy as one might think.

Not only is it next to impossible to disprove the legitimacy of a service-dog team but also the risks of attempting to do so far outweigh the rewards. For example, if employees suspect that a person entering their place of business alongside a dog is fraudulently doing so, they are legally allowed to ask the above two questions—which a person who is passing off his/her pet as a service dog will answer falsely without compunction. The business owner or employees must then decide whether to ask the individual and his/her dog to leave.

> Recently a disabled veteran was turned away from a well-known national fast-food-chain restaurant because of the presence of his service dog. A storm on social media followed. This is not an unusual occurrence. It happens often.

It is very risky for businesses to deny access to people with service dogs even when they suspect that those dogs are merely pets. If they do so, and the service-dog team proves to be legitimate, they face civil penalties and fines upwards of $55,000 per offense. This said, management does have the protection of asking an individual to remove an ill-behaved or disruptive dog from the premises.

Some people believe that they have a right to take their dogs with them wherever they go. Places where dogs were traditionally not permitted are forced to look the other way due to the potential repercussions of denying entry to a service dog.

> *IT IS AGAINST FEDERAL LAW* to represent your dog as a service animal if he is not. There is a large fine and jail time involved, not to mention how unfair it is to those people who really need their service dogs in order to maintain their quality of life.

How can restaurant employees, for example, know the difference between a real service dog and a fake service dog? They can't. And that is the heart of the problem.

It could be argued that the majority of people who pass off their pets as service dogs are not doing so with ill intent. Instead, they are simply trying to spend more time with the dogs they love. However, these people do not consider the effects of their actions.

Legitimate service dogs are highly trained, incredibly well mannered, and under the complete control of their handlers at all times whereas fake service dogs are often disruptive—they haven't had the hundreds of hours of training and socialization required to function as service dogs.

Likewise, their handlers often lack control over their dogs and don't respond appropriately when their access to public places is challenged—whereas an experienced handler with full knowledge of rights and responsibilities would know what to do and say.

As a result, fake service-dog teams create discrimination toward legitimate teams. A business owner who has dealt with unruly behavior from a "faker" may pass judgment on a true service-dog team the very minute they walk through the door. This discrimination leads to poor or even unlawful treatment of legitimate service-dog teams in a variety of ways such as isolating them in an empty part of a restaurant, ignoring them, failing to serve them, following them around in a store, etc.

Further, fake service dogs pose a safety hazard not present with true service dogs. While service dogs are predictable, reliable, and trained to remain calm, quiet, and out of the way in a variety of circumstances, a family pet disguised as a service dog is most often not so reliable, making him a threat both to other patrons and to real service dogs that may enter the premises.

Disabled people already face bias or discrimination on a regular basis. The recent proliferation of fake service-dog teams has created a culture in which business owners and employees, more often than not, are suspicious of all service-dog teams. Instead of assuming that most are legitimate and a rare few are fake, they assume that most are fake and very few are real.

Legal Protections

By law, service dogs have access to apartments, condominiums, stores, restaurants, hospitals, doctors' offices, movie theaters, sports arenas, or anywhere that a person is normally allowed to go. However, here are some tips:

➤ **Apartments**: An apartment complex with fewer than four units is NOT bound by federal law regarding service dogs. But if there are four or more units, service dogs must be allowed—no matter the size or breed. The management may request that the dog be "dressed" when in public areas— wearing a vest and identifying patches. We recommend complying with such requests to maintain good relations.

➤ **Condominiums**: Homeowners' associations (five units or more) are required to allow service dogs.

➤ **Hotels**: Required to allow service dogs without surcharge.

➤ **Stores**: Required to allow service dogs.

➤ **Restaurants**: Required to allow service dogs.

22

> ➢ **Doctors' offices/hospitals**: Required to allow service dogs.
> ➢ **Public transportation**: Required to allow service dogs (some cabbies object—let it go!).

Where May a Service Dog Go?

A service dog is allowed to go wherever a person is allowed. However, we consider it unfair to force the dog to be in a place where he is uncomfortable. He may be legally permitted to be there, but that doesn't mean that he *should* be there. For example, our dog doesn't enjoy movies because there is almost always a loud sound, cars crashing, shots fired, or screaming—so he stays home when we go to movies or plays.

Audrey Hepburn with her deer

It is certainly best to do what you can to avoid confrontations.

When going out in public, it is good etiquette to be sure that your dog is "dressed" in a vest with identifying patches, and you should carry his service-dog ID card. This is especially important to business and store owners so that other customers know why your dog is allowed and theirs isn't.

In many countries around the world, disabled individuals with assistance dogs are guaranteed legal access to all places of public accommodation, modes of public transportation, recreation, and other places where the general public is allowed. Service-dog handlers who are planning foreign travel should carefully research the laws and customs of the countries they intend to visit. We recommend the U.S.

Department of State website sections on international travel and also the website www.servicedogcentral.org.

If your service dog does not behave appropriately in public, the owner, proprietor, or manager of a business or facility may ask you to leave. Having a service dog does not exempt you from the responsibility to follow basic standards of polite public behavior. If your child were running around and screaming like a Tasmanian devil, you would be asked to leave, too!

Keep in mind that some people are allergic to dogs—and some people are afraid of dogs. You do not have the right to terrorize others. Be sensitive and be accommodating.

Choosing Your Dog

Once you have decided that you need a service dog and have concluded that you have the space for a dog and are physically and financially able to care for one, how do you find a dog? There are many ways to acquire a service dog. Choose the method that is most comfortable for you.

Where Can I Get a Service Dog?

There are many places to get a dog:

- Agency or organization
- Shelter

- Breeder or kennel

If you are considering an adult dog, find out why this dog is available. We recommend having a service-dog trainer evaluate the dog before you commit.

Agencies and Organizations

An agency will provide you with a fully trained dog and will match you and the dog on a personal level. You must apply to receive a dog, and the agency will determine whether you qualify. Standards and requirements vary from agency to agency. The wait time may range from three months to five years. Agencies may consider factors such as these:

➤ They may not place a dog in a home where there is another dog or where there are children under age eighteen.

➤ They may require that you live in a home with a yard and not in an apartment or condo.

➤ Some organizations retain ownership of the dog and, in effect, lease him to you.

➤ Some organizations require follow-up training and welfare checks of the service animals that they provide. This is a real benefit because people tend to relax maintenance of the dog's skills over time and agency checks will keep the dog performing at peak efficiency.

If you're uncomfortable with an agency's guidelines or policies, don't argue or expect them to change their rules for you. Just move on to another organization. There are so many agencies and organizations that you will find one that meets your needs.

Many agencies maintain their own breeding programs and breed dogs specifically for temperament and intelligence. The most common are Labrador Retrievers or Golden Retrievers—breeds that tend to be calm and stable.

Agencies and organizations invest money, time, and the love and dedication of their employees in every dog that they provide. Most agencies have not only paid staff but also many volunteers—puppy raisers, kennel personnel, and trainers. Most people who receive service dogs never know how much work and love went into the training of their animals. We cannot say enough about the special people who staff these organizations, except to say "thank you."

How to Find an Agency: Agencies can be found in almost every state. It is important to take your time and find an organization or agency that is a good fit for you. We recommend relying on word of mouth—a support group, a social worker, an online search. Each agency has its own specific criteria, target clientele, geographic span, and special interests. To make a match with a provider organization, you need to become familiar with the various organizations.

The International Association of Assistance Dog Partners (www.iaadp.org), Canine Companions for Independence (www.cci.org), and Pet Partners (formerly Delta Society [www.deltasociety.org]) are just three of them. Start locally, and then expand to national organizations if necessary.

You will be required to submit an application and other supportive materials when applying for a service dog. Be prepared—it takes time, and there may be a long waiting list.

Shelters

Many good service dogs come from shelters, but you must ask these questions to determine whether you can find a suitable dog in this environment:

- Why is the dog in the shelter? Does he have bad habits? Eat shoes, eat the kids?
- How long has he been there—three days, three weeks, three months?
- What type of facility is this shelter—clean and spacious or dungeon-like and nasty?

In addition, you must find out whether the dog has been in a crate for an extended period of time or has ever been abused. Dogs who have been crated or abused seldom overcome the resultant mental problems. Your dog must be able to take care of you in all social circumstances—and you must be able to rely on your dog.

You are not selecting a "pet" but rather a companion on whom you will depend in more ways than you can imagine. Let the dog choose you. Set up a situation in which the dog you like will seek you out and want to be close to you. Shelter dogs can become wonderful working dogs, but investigation in advance may save you much distress.

If you decide to get a dog from a shelter or rescue organization, take along a service-dog trainer to make an evaluation. Paying a trainer for an hour of his/her time may save you many frustrating hours of trying to train a dog that may not work out. This is so important; service-dog trainers know what qualities a dog must possess for service work.

After a trainer locates a candidate for you, find out if that dog likes you. We believe the dog should choose you. In other words, the dog should want to be with you. You will know if the dog likes you, and you will definitely know if the dog doesn't like you. Don't pick the first dog that the trainer says fits the bill—go to several shelters and search. Remember that this dog will be your working partner—he will be with you twenty-four hours a day for every day of his life and yours.

Dog Breeders and Breeds

Breeders come in all forms: bad, good, better, and best. Dogs are bred for service work according to a specific set of guidelines for such factors as size, temperament, and intelligence. These qualities are bred into a dog's bloodline by years of selection.

To locate a breeder, decide on the breed of dog that you want. The best breed for you is the breed that you like and that fits your living circumstances and physical limitations. Visit the kennel and ask for references.

The most popular service-dog breeds are the Golden Retriever and Labrador Retriever. Samoyeds, Smooth Collies, and Rough Collies are becoming more popular. Some of the more unusual breeds assisting disabled handlers are Pointers, Otterhounds, Dalmatians, Irish Setters, Papillons, and Greyhounds—even pit bulls, showing that you can't always judge a book by its cover.

Some of the factors that you should consider in selecting a breed are:

Size: A hearing-assist, medical-assist, or emotional-support dog may be any size. If you are selecting a breed for mobility assistance or seizure assistance, identify a very knowledgeable breeder who can accurately predict what size his/her pups will be at maturity.

As a rule, a service dog should stand a minimum of 22 inches and weigh a minimum of 55 pounds for wheelchair-assistance work, if pulling a child or a small woman. For adults weighing over 130 pounds, the dog should weigh 60 pounds or more. Dogs trained for balance support typically are a minimum of 23 inches tall for an average-sized woman, if a harness with a sturdy handle tall enough to bridge the gap between the human's hand and the dog's withers is available. If an ordinary harness, minus handle, is used for balance support, a much taller dog is needed—27 to 30 inches tall so that the person's hand can rest on the dog's back.

Longevity: Another factor to investigate is the average lifespan of a breed. For example, the majority of Bernese Mountain Dogs only live for about six years. Most large breeds have a ten- to twelve-year lifespan. Small- and medium-sized dogs might live well into their teens. One giant breed has a lifespan of only four years, while another averages ten years. It is unwise to make assumptions. Research before you take the plunge.

Lifestyle: When selecting a breed, think about where you live and your lifestyle. Are you in the working world? A student? Retired? Do you live in a home with a yard, a condo, an apartment? Maybe you are traveling the country in a recreational vehicle. The dog's size will in itself tell you how much exercise is needed.

Allergies: If you are allergic to dogs, or someone in your family is allergic, look into breeds that have fur, not hair—for example, Poodles or Poodle blends such as Labradoodles (Labrador/Poodle mix) or Goldendoodles (Golden Retriever/Poodle mix). Portuguese Water Dogs are also hypoallergenic.

Care: An important consideration in breed choice is your physical ability and/or financial ability to manage the grooming needs of a particular breed. Some long-haired breeds may require a weekly two-hour-long comb-out. Some breeds require only intermittent brushing. A breed with a hypoallergenic coat, such as a Standard Poodle, will need weekly comb-outs and regular visits to a professional grooming shop. A short-haired breed, such as a Labrador Retriever, will only need weekly brushing and a bath once or twice per year to remain healthy. Shorter hair does not mean less shedding; daily shedding is probable year round.

Hereditary Breed Traits: Each breed was developed for a purpose. If you are considering a breed developed for hunting, herding, or guard work, realize that the traits which made that particular breed an excellent hunting dog, an effective sheepdog, or a successful guard dog do not disappear just because these traits are no longer desired by most dog owners. The ancestral urges to hunt, swim, chase livestock, sound an alarm, kill predators, or drive away strangers are lurking beneath the surface. Some of these traits may interfere with a service dog's reliability.

Age: One of the most important decisions to make is whether to start out with a puppy or seek an adult dog (age eighteen months to three years) that can commence train-ing immediately.

The Search: When searching for a breeder, let your fingers do the walking. Search engines are great; start with Google, then Yahoo, then Bing. They will show different results, so use them all—it's free! Enter the breed of dog you are in-terested in, research information about that breed, then search for organizations and clubs for that specific breed. You can find organizations and clubs for every breed of dog. You should find several breeders advertising on each of the club or organization websites that you locate. Usually members of the organization or club will know the breed-ers, so take time to ask for recommendations.

It is also worth looking into rescue dogs for the breed that you choose. Be sure that your choice does not have drawbacks that make it an undesirable choice.

"No matter how little money and how few possessions you own, having a dog makes you rich."
—Louis Sabin

PART II

Public Access

Where May I Take My Dog?

A service dog in the United States may go anywhere that a human is allowed to go with few exceptions. Those exceptions are noteworthy for common-sense reasons: no public-restaurant kitchens, no spas, no sterile operating rooms, etc.

We don't take our service dog to the zoo for obvious reasons.

When in Tennessee, we visited the family-owned George Dickel distillery, founded in the 1860s. We were politely asked not to take Snow Prince on the public tour because the machines were not modern, encapsulated equipment.

The employees were so nice about it; they gave Wayne and

Snow Prince a private tour and answered many questions. When we visited the Coors factory in Denver, it was a state-of-the-art facility and we were allowed to take the dog with us on the public tour. It is important to keep perspective and to be conscious of others' needs.

When we are told that someone in our vicinity is allergic to dogs, we always move in order to act in the best interest of all.

The same holds true if your dog is behaving inappropriately or disruptively. In a restaurant your dog should lie quietly under the table near your feet until you are ready to leave; on a travel conveyance, in an office—the same. Landlords also reserve the right to evict you if you violate their rules regarding proper behavior.

You are NOT expected to pay a surcharge for your dog in hotels, on cruise ships, in airplanes, or on other modes of transportation.

Questions, Questions, Everywhere . . .

Yes, oh yes—everywhere you go there will be questions:

- What's his name?
- What breed is he?
- What does he do for you?
- Where does he go to the bathroom?

On and on . . . it never ends. People will also want to stop you to tell you about *their* dog and show you a picture of their dog. It may seem odd, it may be annoying, but remember that these people are trying to connect with you in a compassionate way.

At first you will be patient and kind. After hundreds of these requests you will begin to get impatient. But you CANNOT do that. By having a service dog you are putting yourself out there, and it is incumbent upon you to try to educate people. What these dogs do and how they do it is fascinating to people. Sometimes a person will approach you because he/she needs a service dog and doesn't know where to start.

Responding kindly will make your interactions with the public so much easier. Once you learn to answer people patiently, you will find that there is no frustration for either of you. And remember that, every time you face this challenge, your dog feels it. If you stress out, your dog will become anxious and fearful because he senses these emotions in you. If you remain calm and can take these incidents in stride, so will your dog.

You would be surprised to learn how often people interrupt us while we're dining and spend a lot of time talking to us about our dog. The same happens when we are on our way somewhere; we don't want to be rude, but we also don't want to be late for where we are going. People just don't think, and they are all curious about the dog. And, of course, they all want to share. These people mean well, but they don't understand that you are not a sideshow. In our case, since our business is service-dog related, we make extra effort to be patient and to spend time so that we can educate people.

Like it or not, once you partner with a service dog you become an advocate for service dogs. You can choose to embrace that role in any style you prefer, or you can be angry and life will be harder. People just want to understand all the things that your dog can do for you, and they are amazed by the dog's ability to be so smart!

Identification

As of 2015, it is not the law that your dog must wear identifying dress such as a vest and patches. But it is very considerate to any establishment that you're entering to let staff and other patrons know why the dog is there. This is especially true of places that do not normally allow dogs to enter—others will wonder why their dogs can't come in while yours can.

There will be times when you are challenged—when people are confrontational or argumentative. Having your dog properly dressed will eliminate most of them.

It may not be easy to get a vest on your dog in the beginning. He may find having something put over his head to be unnerving.

Once he understands what is happening to him and that it does not hurt, he should start to push his head through the opening of his vest and stand still so that it can be buckled under his belly.

The vest should fit like a saddle and not strangle him around the neck. When he gets used to wearing the vest—which should not take long at all—he will begin to look forward to putting it on because it signals that he is about to go out and do his job—much like putting on a business suit! He knows that he will not be left at home and that he is working. The first time he readily adapts to wearing the vest, you should praise him and reinforce with pets or a treat.

We cannot tell you how many times we have had people call our offices to say that some business or public

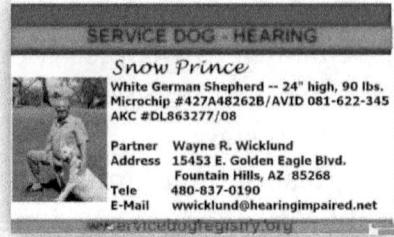

building wouldn't let their service dog in. Almost invariably in these situations, the dog has not been wearing a vest or patches.

Yes, federal law mandates that a business must let your service dog in even without identifying dress. But it is foolish to think that a restaurant or any business other than a pet store will welcome your dog without proper identifying dress.

Restaurants are worried about being cited for health-code violations if they let your dog in without his being properly identified as a service dog.

If your dog is not correctly dressed, you are going to have a hassle anywhere you go. To avoid this, put on the dog's proper dress when going out in public and enjoy your day!

What do you need? We recommend a service-dog vest or harness, a service-dog ID card with photos of you and your dog, a collar, and a leash that has "Service Dog" imprinted on it.

If you have all those things, your chances of being hassled are really remote.

Certification

Yes, you can certify your dog. This is done by a designated trainer or evaluator. As of 2015, it is NOT the law that your dog must be certified. It is still a good idea if that option is available to you. Trainers and evaluators who can certify are sometimes hard to find, depending on where you live. An internet search would be a good place to start.

A common misconception about service dogs is that registration or licensing is required by law. According to the ADA, it is illegal for businesses to request documentation before granting a service dog and handler access to a facility: "Staff cannot ask about the person's disability, require medical documentation, require a special identification card or training documentation for the dog, or ask that the dog demonstrate its ability to perform the work or task."

The important distinction here is that a handler may provide documentation if he/she chooses to do so, but businesses are not supposed to expect it.

Being Apart

Do I have to take the dog everywhere all the time? … **Yes**
May I leave the dog at home sometimes? … **Yes**

There are no hard-and-fast rules. If the dog does not accompany you almost everywhere you go, then you don't really need him and he will lose training. On the other hand, if you don't leave him at home sometimes he will suffer separation anxiety when you *do* leave him.

Quite a dilemma. You can figure this out. There are times when it will be inappropriate to take the dog.

If, for example, you are in the hospital you may find it necessary to have someone else take care of your dog. You should prepare for this in advance. Wayne has a friend who is the *only* person allowed to give Shadow food and take Shadow home with him. Should we need to call on this friend to care for Shadow, he and the dog will be comfortable with each other and ready. You need to make those preparations.

Overwhelmed by Crowds

We know—we know! It is almost unbearable to go into a restaurant or a mall when *everyone* wants to pet your

dog or wants to talk with you for what seems like hours. You are in a hurry to get to your destination and get out, or you want to relax and enjoy an afternoon with family or friends. But everywhere you go, people are curious. They want to know:

- What breed is your dog?
- How old is he?
- What's his name?
- What does he do for you?
- How do you train him?
- Where does he go to the bathroom?

At first it's kind of fun, interesting, and entertaining. But after awhile it just gets old. You marvel at how rude people are. Can't they see you're in a hurry? Or trying to eat a meal?

And *everyone* wants to tell you about his or her dog!

> We traveled with three other people to Washington, D.C. for a convention. As part of the activities, we visited various memorials. While at the Lincoln Memorial we were surrounded by Japanese tourists wanting to take pictures of our dog, Snow Prince. Wayne never did get to see or enjoy the memorial because we had a tour bus to catch—so, it happens to all of us.

Our answer to this is to simply chill. Take a deep breath because it is never going to stop. The more you fight it, the more frustrating it will become for you.

People are so very interested in service dogs and how they work—how the dogs know *how* to do what they do! The public simply cannot get enough. People see a service dog so perfectly behaved and wonder how to get *their* dogs to behave that well. They have no idea how much training goes into making this excellent behavior seem effortless. Here are some strategies for fending off the curious without insulting them:

> **Please don't pet him, he's working**. Many people will see the "Do Not Pet" patch on your dog's vest and say, "I know I shouldn't pet him" while they are petting the dog! You could explain that, if your dog is distracted, he will lose his focus and will forget to help you. Usually that short explanation works.

> **I would love to talk with you more, but I really am in a hurry for an appointment.** As you quickly walk away, you've ended the conversation without offending anyone.

> **I would love to stay and chat with you, but please excuse me—I am eager to see this exhibit.** No one can get angry when you politely excuse yourself from a conversation.

Recently Anne was talking with a woman who suggested raising your hand in a "stop" gesture, reaching into your pocket, producing a preprinted card with various answers, and then walking away. It is not recommended, but it is an alternative.

Take a minute if you can to be a good, positive ambassador on behalf of all service-dog teams. It's so much easier than getting angry yourself or offending others.

You will find that authority figures such as police officers are not always knowledgeable about service dogs—strange, but true! You have the opportunity to educate them courteously.

For people with emotional issues or PTSD, going out in public with their services dogs can be even more challenging because they risk potential interactions that could restimulate painful past events.

DO NOT UPSET YOURSELF is the bottom line. As Dear Abby wrote to a service-dog handler who complained about the barrage of questions, "you must be realistic . . . you must accept that people will be curious. However, what many people fail to understand is that when a service dog is out in public, the animal is working and should not be distracted from its task—which is ensuring the well being of the owner."[2]

How to Say "NO!"

We often attend conventions of ten thousand people or more. The first thing

---

[2] Jeanne Phillips, "Dear Abby: Owner: Leave service dog alone," *The Arizona Republic*, April 11, 2014, accessed June 19, 2015,
http://www.azcentral.com/story/life/2014/04/11/dear-abby-owner-leave-service-dog-alone/7621547/

we do is to make sure that Shadow is properly dressed in his vest or harness with identifying patches.

Most people have the idea that, if a service dog is well marked, they may ask to pet him. Wayne usually tells them politely that "the dog is working right now and he has to focus on his job; however, if you see me outside and the dog has his vest or harness off, then the dog knows it is free time and he can be friendly to the people around him." Wayne explains that, for the dog, there is a difference between work time and play time.

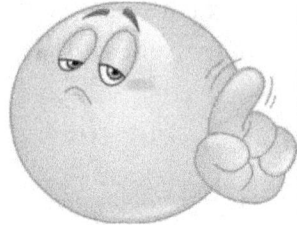

To Pet or Not to Pet

Whether you let people pet your dog is your option. But the rule is that it is NEVER all right to pet a service dog. There are several reasons why this is so:

- 🐾 Your dog should focus on you and the sounds and smells surrounding you. Your bodily odors tell the dog if you are in distress, and the dog's focus should not be interrupted by strangers petting him.
- 🐾 You need to protect your dog from overstimulation. Dogs are not used to being in crowds, and they can find crowds threatening. If you take your dog to Costco, WalMart, or the town fair, you're asking him to process a multitude of strange smells and sounds simultaneously while also protecting you. Don't overburden him by allowing strangers to pet him.
- 🐾 That said, there are some exceptions. We let our dog receive attention from:

- o **Children** (well behaved). This teaches children not to fear dogs and educates them.
- o **Elderly people**. Petting a dog calms people.
- o **Autistic people**. The petting ritual can help them connect with others. But be sure that the autistic individual is ready to allow you into his/her space.

Something else that we do in large crowds is to attach two blinking diode lights (similar to what bicycle riders wear at night) to the top of the dog's vest. When you are walking in crowds, you quickly learn that people are in a hurry getting around and they don't look down. They will walk right over your dog, not knowing that he is walking next to you below their line of sight. You could also attach a little flag that is a couple of feet high to your dog's harness. This catches people's attention and can prevent them from stepping on or tripping over your dog.

We also walk with the dog between us so that he is protected from both sides.

In large crowds, your dog will struggle to avoid being stepped on and this is very stressful for him. When we are at conventions or in other large crowds, we take frequent breaks in a snack area or other spot where Shadow can lie down at Wayne's feet, protected by a table over him.

If you are out all day with your dog, he will need several relief breaks. Be sure that you know where you can take him to relieve himself. Always remember to carry water for your dog. We carry a portable container that folds up into the dog's vest and sometimes a large, flat-bottomed Thermos container.

People ask to pet your dog because: (1) they like dogs, (2) your dog stands out because he is dressed in service-dog work attire, and (3) they are curious. Sometimes people want to learn how your dog helps you because they or someone they love could benefit from having a service dog.

People usually stop and ask to pet your dog or want to talk about your dog at the most inconvenient times! You may be in a hurry, getting the dog out of the car, or feeling ill or tired. For Wayne it is usually when he is sick and trying to get somewhere. He tells himself, "You are always sick, so cheer up and try to be extra friendly and helpful."

He always remembers that we are ambassadors for service animals. And he remembers when he was one of those people asking the questions. When someone asks you for information, try to bear in mind that you could be the person who gives that someone the courage to get a service dog that could change his or her life—or the life of a family member or friend—for the better.

Your dog will always know when someone around you is sick. Sometimes people look like they are in good health, when in fact they have serious illnesses. When people first see Wayne, they think he looks great; but, after just a few minutes, they realize that he has major physical problems. If Shadow stops and pays attention to someone, Wayne knows that this person is probably ill and lets his dog say "hi." He has found, in the course of talking with these people, that they often mention they have health problems. Wayne can walk into any room where there are service dogs, and they will all come up to him and try to assist him in their own way. Many people who are partnered with service dogs have experienced this.

Shopping Malls

Yes, indeed—here they come again—the hordes of people who are insatiably curious about your service dog! They will stop you everywhere to ask: Why do you have a service dog? What breed is it? May I pet it?

Your choice is to be patient and give them as much time as you choose or to be kind but cut it short. Say, "I'm sorry, but I'm in a hurry." That should do it. Usually you won't have a problem with mall security personnel; they just want to be sure that the dog is truly a service animal and is properly behaved and dressed. They are *required* to ask—so don't lose patience.

You may want to park near an area where your dog can relieve himself before going into the mall. Make sure that you have his working equipment on—his harness or vest plus identification.

Inside the mall, you know that every little kid is going to want to pet your dog. That's what kids do. If your dog is properly trained, he will be friendly but aloof—he will not really pay any attention because he will be focused on helping you.

The exception to this is, of course, a sight dog. They follow a completely different set of guidelines. A sight dog should never be touched or distracted in any way while working.

Safety Advice: When walking in a mall, you will encounter many different types of people. It's up to you to decide how you want to allow them to interact with your dog. Some guidelines:

➢ If someone wants to pet your dog, only let him/her pet from the top of the dog's shoulders, going along the top of the back for about eight inches.

➢ Put your hand next to his/hers and never let him/her go towards the dog's head. Tell people before they begin to pet the dog that they cannot pet toward his head because the dog must always be able to see what is going on around him.

➢ Sometimes a person will very quickly slide his/her hand up along the dog's ear and squeeze it. This is painful, so never let a stranger pet your dog without your hand right above his/hers.

➢ Petting your dog, with your hand on top of his/her hand, can help a child get over a fear of dogs.

Restaurants

As long as your dog behaves appropriately and is not disruptive, he will be legally allowed inside any restaurant. Some restaurant owners and managers do not know this. How could they *not* know?!! But they don't. So—once again, you may have to calmly educate and let them know it is the law.

Choose a table out of the way, against a wall, in a corner. You don't want a server to trip over the dog. Your table should be away from the kitchen and the wait station, and your dog should be quietly lying on the floor under the table. You are going to have a very uptight dog on your hands if he is worried about being stepped on or having something spilled on him.

We know of a woman who lives in Las Vegas and uses a power wheelchair. Her service dog is a Papillon named Cooper. She entered a restaurant and saw the manager bearing toward her. She waited until the manager was almost to her, and then noisily dropped her keys. "Oops!" she said, using one of her secret cue words for her dog to pick up the object. Her dog immediately responded, picked up the keys, assumed a "paws up" position with his front paws on the edge of her wheelchair, and held the keys in his mouth until she was ready to take them.

Before the manager could speak, she continued with her people training. "This little dog also makes my bed and does the laundry. I don't know what I'd do without him." It was worth the two years of training, she said, to get her dog to his skill level.

The manager remained mute and a bit stunned to learn that this fluff ball was a service dog. Like many business owners, he had probably never seen a legitimate service dog this small.

The woman then said with a twinkle in her eye, "Here, watch how he'll get my cell phone!" The manager escorted them to their table—another convert to the world of small service dogs.

Your dog should never ever beg for food from the table or be given food from the table. If a dog is given food from the table at home, he will not understand that it is forbidden in a restaurant. Like Snow Prince before him, Shadow never gets "people food," so he doesn't want or desire it. If you do choose to give your dog green beans, cottage cheese, rice, or other "people food," place the food in the dog's food bowl at home.

47

Choose your time of day according to how busy or noisy the restaurant will be. If you arrive just before or just after the mealtime rush, you can usually find a good table that suits your needs and your dog's. If the host or hostess is young and inexperienced, he or she may want to seat you at a table that is totally inappropriate. For instance, with our very large dog we need a larger, out-of-the-way table. Always talk with the host or hostess and ask him/her to show you the table.

If your dog is disruptive or otherwise causes problems in a restaurant, you may be asked to leave and it is the restaurateur's right.

If you are asked to leave a restaurant or denied access for no apparent reason, your remedy is to:

- Explain the law
- Call the police
- File a complaint with your state's attorney general
- File a complaint with the U.S. Department of Justice

To avoid conflicts, confrontations, and embarrassment, always have your dog identifiable as a service dog by using a vest or harness and identifying patches. And have your service-dog ID handy.

Dinner Engagements

We are very active in our community and often attend dinners with fifty to one hundred people in attendance, a meeting, and a speaker. We usually know ahead of time who will be seated with us. We arrive half an hour in advance to scout out a good location and confirm that Shadow has everything he needs to be comfortable and be able to lie still for the duration of the event. Wayne makes sure that seating arrangements are settled, and then he takes the dog outside for a relief break before the activities start. We make sure to feed Shadow before we leave home. If you, too, do this type of preparation, it will ensure that you have a nice, relaxing time and that your dog is happy and content.

If event seating is at large, round banquet tables, this is perfect for either a large or a small dog. When we are seated at these types of tables, Wayne sits where there is no folding leg and lifts the tablecloth so that Shadow can lie under the table facing outward and can see everything going on around him. Wayne takes the dog for his relief break during each break in the activity (the dog first, and then Wayne).

When being entertained in someone's home, be sure to verify in advance with your host or hostess whether it is all right to bring your dog. Some people are allergic, some do NOT want a dog in their homes (dog hair, etc.), and some have other pets that may make it difficult. Be sensitive to others' needs and be prepared to leave your dog at home for a few hours unless having him with you is essential to your well being.

Entertainment and Events

The law states that a service dog is entitled to go wherever you go. Our Snow Prince *loved* to go to the theater—he liked plays and movies.

But we quickly found that, even though we were well accommodated by the community theater in our town, almost every play includes loud noises, gunshots, screaming, foot stomping, running up and down the aisle, etc. This was intolerable to Snow—why make him suffer just because the law says he can be there? We found the same to be true of movies, but that could be because Wayne only wants to see movies that involve blood, guts, and bombing—lots of action flicks. Snow Prince was more of a romantic!

Behavior

Just as you are expected to behave in a certain way in public, so is your dog. You cannot reasonably be offended by an objection if your dog is sniffing food on tables, sitting in a chair intended for humans, or blocking a doorway. While in a restaurant, at an event, or in a private home, your dog should lie quietly under the table or next to you where he is out of the way and servers cannot trip on him. People should not even be aware that a dog is there until you leave and they see the dog rise from his down position. It's always fun to see the surprise on people's faces!

Anywhere that you go, your dog is allowed to go by federal law. But use common sense, plan ahead, and be sure that your dog is comfortable, well provided for, and behaves appropriately.

To Work/School

Yes—you may take your dog to work and to school, but that doesn't necessarily mean that you *should*. Think about your schedule. Think about whether your colleagues can accommodate themselves to your dog's needs. You want the cooperation of those around you. If you are highly mobile during the work or school day, it may not be a good idea to have your dog with you. If you sit at a desk most of the day and have the opportunity to take your dog for relief breaks, it may work well. Think about the severity of your needs and use your good judgment when you make a request to the administration.

To Work: Wayne's service dog is with him almost one hundred percent of the time. In our office the dog is always with him, and our employees are allowed to bring their dogs to work. Of course, there are often dogs in our office since we make service-dog supplies. We find that having a dog in the office usually makes a happier office and helps relieve stress.

Per the ADA, companies with fifteen or more employees must allow service dogs to accompany their handlers. Small companies—defined by the ADA as those with fourteen or fewer employees—are exempt from this requirement, at management's discretion.

Over the years, in talking with many disabled people, we've found that most companies gladly accommodate employees with service dogs.

Is it necessary for you to have your dog with you at work? Talk it over with your superiors so that they understand what your dog does for you and how important this may be to your well being. Be ready to compromise.

Consider these factors:

➢ Do you have the time and ability to take your dog for exercise during the work day?

➢ Do you have the time and ability to take him for relief breaks?

➢ Do you have the time and ability to give him food
and water?

➢ Feeding his dog has been the easiest task for Wayne.
He always makes sure that he has Shadow's food and
treats with him, plus a jug of water with ice cubes in
it. (Wayne lives in the Desert Southwest, and his dog
insists on having nice cool water on his breaks!)

➢ No matter how well you plan your day, things
change. Wayne often finds that he has to rearrange a
meeting time or location. Having Shadow's food,
water, and other essential items with him allows
Wayne to be flexible.

If you are looking for a job, take the following points
into consideration:

➢ You will get a feeling in your first interview as to
whether the company really wants you *and* your dog because it will be clear that you are a package deal (you and
your working partner).

➢ Before your interview, look around outside the office or factory and see whether there is a convenient place
to give your dog a relief break. Think about how far it is
from where you would be working to the relief area for
your dog because you must not only give your dog breaks
but also give yourself breaks as well, and this takes time
away from your desk or work area. For Wayne, the distance
to the relief area for his dog is important because there are
days when he has a very hard time walking. If there are
times when it is too difficult for you to take your dog for a
relief break, would it be permissible for you to ask someone
in the office who likes dogs to take your dog out? These

types of questions must be considered when you apply for a job.

➢ It is important to know what the sound level will be in any potential work environment. Since one of Wayne's problems is hearing, he doesn't always know if the sound in an area is too much for the dog. Shadow lets him know when the sound is too loud, and they leave that area.

Your dog and your attending to your dog's needs should not interfere with your employer's normal course of business. It is not fair to expect that.

To School: The same guidelines that apply to a work situation apply at school.

Some schools try to prevent young children from having their service dogs at school because a teacher fears that the dog's presence may disrupt the classroom. This should be challenged by the child's parents or guardian, who may file complaints with the state attorney general, the U.S. Department of Justice, and the local school board.

Never let anyone or any business or organization abuse you as a disabled person or abuse a child or other family member who is disabled. There are advocates and agencies that will help protect your rights if you are unable to do so for yourself.

Service dogs may become overstressed in a school setting, with many active children distracting them from their work. Teachers and staff can help by emphasizing that this

is not a pet but a working dog that provides needed assistance to the disabled child.

Parents or guardians should consult with the school's administration and staff about whether it is appropriate for the child's service dog to accompany him/her at school— carefully considering the disability and the age of the child in question.

Hospitals and Medical Offices

Yes, your dog is allowed in— however, let's be clear. If there is a contagion, contamination, or immunity issue, **NOT**. If someone in the vicinity is allergic to dogs or afraid of your dog, please be considerate and leave. If you are hospitalized your dog may visit but should be accompanied by a caretaker.

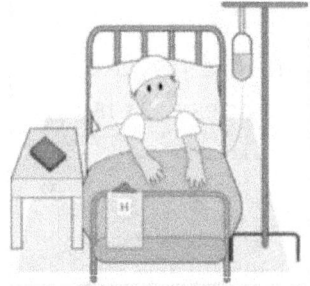

Hospitals: Many hospitals have therapy-dog programs and are happy to have dogs in the facility. Doctors' offices can be iffy, but there should be no real problem if you use discretion and good manners.

You shouldn't have any difficulty entering hospitals if your dog is dressed for his job. However, if your dog is not in his service vest you will not be allowed in. You can argue the federal law all you want, but it's easier to just make sure that your service dog is wearing his work outfit and save yourself a lot of problems.

There are some places in a hospital where you can't take your dog:

> **You cannot take your dog into an operating room or x-ray room** unless the room is set up for a service dog to be there. For example, some VA hospitals serve so many patients with service dogs that they have set up areas near the x-ray tables where dogs can sit behind protective glass and see their partners while tests or treatment are in progress.

"Which arrow points to my office?"

> **Your dog cannot be in an area of the hospital that handles immune deficiencies.** Sometimes your dog will not be allowed in the intensive-care unit (ICU), where patients often have compromised immune systems. However, Wayne has had several extended stays in ICUs and in each instance Anne was allowed to bring his dog daily, taking the dog home at night since hospital staff could not be expected to take the dog out for relief breaks.

Wayne has been in many hospitals across the United States and Canada and has never had any problems taking his service dog with him, as long as the dog had on his service-dog vest, collar, leash, or work equipment.

Medical Offices: Going to medical offices is the same as going to the hospital. As long as your dog is wearing his service-dog vest, harness, etc., you should not have any problems.

When Wayne sees his allergist, he must be isolated in a room at the back of the clinic because other patients are sometimes allergic to dogs. After Wayne leaves, clinic employees clean the room thoroughly. To save them this inconvenience Wayne often leaves the dog at home when visiting this particular doctor.

Theme Parks

It's fun to take the dog to a theme park! At first he may be nervous because of the crowds, but he will adjust. If your dog is small, you might want to carry him in a sling so that he doesn't get hurt (no strollers, please). If he is a large dog, he can walk. Be sure the dog is wearing his shoes or boots if it is a hot day; this

Snow Prince enjoying the tram ride at Disneyland

also protects him from sticky or sharp objects that people may drop on the ground.

Be prepared for all the people who will be curious about your dog, want to pet him, etc.

There will be rides that are inappropriate: roller coasters, Ferris wheels, spinning or looping rides. Your dog will probably enjoy the river-cruise type of rides. If he finds the crowds, noise, and flashing lights to be a bit overwhelming, simply limit your activities.

Snow Prince accompanied Wayne several times to Disneyland in California and Disney World in Florida. Snow loved the rides through caves in a log boat, down slides, and through waterfalls!

Airports

You will be able to travel by air with your service dog with relatively few problems. We recommend taking your dog to an airport before you travel to get him accustomed to the sights, sounds, and smells.

We took our dog on the shuttle buses (the brakes freaked him out) and in and out of security screening stations. Some TSA employees may ask you to remove the dog's vest or leash, and some will want the dog to walk through by himself—so be flexible. No two security stations will be exactly alike. If they want to "wand" your dog, be sure this is not done around his head, since that could startle him and make him nervous. Remember that all these experiences are new for your dog and may seem threatening.

You may take your dog into airport restaurants and stores. All airports now have relief areas for service dogs—some are better than others. You will want to let your dog relieve himself immediately before entering the airport and immediately upon leaving. Be sure to give him water since flying is dehydrating.

Most relief areas are not within the secure perimeter, so you will have to go outside to a relief area, then go back inside and through security screening again, then return to your departure gate. If you have a problem with mobility or vision, it will be difficult to get your dog to a relief area. Just ask airport personnel—they will help you.

Airports around the country are working on creating animal-relief areas behind the security entrance so that people with service dogs can avoid repeated trips through security checking.

We recommend that you visit the airport's website before traveling to find out where relief areas are located.

It is sometimes difficult to get to relief areas by wheelchair; if you're in a wheelchair, it will help if you have a traveling companion who can take your dog to relief areas as needed.

Just after you make your reservation, you must advise the airline that you will be accompanied by a service dog. If your dog is small, consider using a carrier to get to and from the plane so that he doesn't get stepped on. If your dog is large, request bulkhead seating in advance.

You may need a health certificate, dated within ten days of your originating flight. International flights and cruise ships require an international health certificate. Your veter-

inarian can provide both types of certificates. Your dog does not have to stay under the seat during an airline flight, and there is no surcharge for traveling with a service dog.

Before foreign travel, you should contact the embassy of each country that you will visit and make sure you have the proper paperwork and health certificates. See these websites for further information: www.pettravel.com and www.aphis.usda.gov/animal_health

The country that you're visiting may quarantine your dog. Remember that laws vary from country to country, and you must comply with them. Never argue with government employees or officials.

We travel to many different countries, and we make sure that we have all necessary documentation for our dog. We check with every official along the way to verify that we have done everything correctly. This makes our international travel easier and more enjoyable.

"Dogs are not our whole life, but they make our lives whole."
—Roger Caras

PART III

Training Your Service Dog

Training Your Own

Yes—you *can* train your own service dog. Converting a pet into a service animal is not as difficult as you may think. Your pet may already be working without your realizing it. The trick is to **listen to your dog**. All animals tell you what they want—for example, when they need to go outside for relief time. But do you realize when your dog is telling you to take your meds? Time for you to eat? Need to lie down because your breathing is not quite right or you are about to have a seizure?

The ADA makes no stipulations about who trains a service dog. And the concept of owner training is growing in popularity as more people realize the benefits of having a service dog.

The $10,000 to $25,000 cost of acquiring a trained service dog is outside the reach of many people, so more and more of them are turning to private trainers to help them train their own service dogs.

A dog of almost any breed can be trained to be a good service dog, although of course you can't expect a Chihuahua to haul you to your feet! You may want to avoid Dobermans, Rottweilers, and pit bulls since they may frighten others—if you're going to take your service dog out in public, you don't want people fleeing from you, running and screaming. On the other hand, we know of at least three pit bulls that are hearing-assist dogs.

Temperament is very important in a service dog. Unless your dog has sociability skills and a balanced disposition, he will never become a good service dog. Once you've determined that your dog has these skills, you may move forward.

There are many trainers who teach people how to train their own dogs for service-dog work. The training process for both handler and dog is extensive. Be sure that the trainer you choose has sufficient background in service-dog training. Carefully interview a trainer about his/her experience with your specific medical condition, length of time as a trainer, and philosophy and techniques of training. Personal attention from a private trainer can be very valuable as preparation, even before a dog is located.

Some trainers prefer to have dogs that are in training wear special vests or other outerwear indicating that the dog is in training. This is optional—not required.

Assistance Dogs International is a great source of information on training.

Self Trained

We are strong proponents of people's training their own service dogs. However, very few people would do what Wayne did—go away to dog-training school, live and work there, and spend thousands of dollars learning how to train a working dog.

If you decide to train your own dog, there are many ways to accomplish this. Most courses take about two years to complete. You usually attend one or two classes each week and then go home to practice what you have learned before the next class. The trainer evaluates your progress along the way to determine whether you and your dog need more training or can advance to the next lesson in your course. To go through this type of training requires a great deal of time, patience, and dedication. There are also many films, books, and websites to help you train.

If you are training a pet to become your service dog, be sure that your dog meets certain basic criteria:

- Has the dog mastered obedience training—sit, stay, down, come, etc?
- Is the dog sociable?
- Does the dog like babies, young children (this cannot be emphasized enough), older children, and adults?

If the answer to any of these questions is "no," you will need to choose another dog. Keep in mind that the first dog may not complete the training. There are many reasons why a dog may be disqualified from service-dog work. Be ready to begin again with a new dog if necessary.

Once you find the perfect dog for you, decide what you want him to do for you aside from providing affection and companionship. Keep in mind:

- ALWAYS make the training fun—it is not rocket science and it shouldn't be stressful for either of you.
- ALWAYS work for short periods of time so neither you nor the dog gets too tired.
- ALWAYS give praise for work done well.
- Most training is simply repetition … repetition … repetition. Just like with kids!

DO NOT let other people feed or give treats to your dog. This would allow people to poison your dog. Or it might enable people to steal your dog (he is valuable).

DO NOT allow your dog to pick up food from the floor unless he put it there (more poison prevention).

If you absolutely cannot stop yourself from giving your dog "people food," make sure that he receives it in his bowl—not from your hand. This will prevent your dog from begging at the table either at home or in public.

Every command that you teach and every problem that you correct will have an impact on all other areas of your dog's behavior. Your dog should be trained to alert you by nudging, pawing, or pulling on the leash. Some dogs alert by spinning in circles or standing still and staring at the offending behavior. How your dog learns to alert will be determined by your training and by his own natural instincts. No one way is right or wrong—the intent is communication. Which command you use is not as important as what you are telling the dog.

If you are unable to speak, you may use sign language; if you can't speak clearly, your dog will still understand you.

Which signal you use is not important as long as you are *consistent* with its meaning.

5 Public Access Skills Every Service Dog Should Know — *by Kea Grace*

One of the most commonly asked questions is, "when is my Service Dog in Training ready for public access?" While that's a question only you or your dog's trainer can answer, here are 5 vital public access skills every Service Dog or Service Dog in Training needs to know before beginning work in public.

Public Access Skills: Down-Stay

A rock-solid down-stay is the mainstay of many Service Dogs' work in public. While there may be brief interludes of task work, many Service Dogs are expected to quietly chill near their handler, under a desk or on a bed until they're expressly needed. A Service Dog needs the ability to quietly relax in any environment without being intrusive, and a down-stay is usually the default method for most handlers and trainers. Service Dogs aren't robots, and some shifting is to be expected, especially if your Service Dog or SDiT is place trained to a mat or bed. That being said, most Service Dogs need to be able to "Under" and "Down Stay" which often blends to the point of being indistinguishable. It must quietly rest for 2 or more hours at a time, which is the length of an average movie, college class or time spent working without a break.

Down stay training begins early, with reinforcement for calm, quiet behavior. Formal "stays" can be taught via many methods, but many people have success with gradually lengthening and rewarding the amount of time their dog spends in one place.

Public Access Skills: Under

"Under" is a behavior that consists of your Service Dog or Service Dog in Training moving fully under a table, bench or chair on cue, with his/her body full tucked beneath the object or your legs as much as if feasibly possible, size depending. The purpose of this public access skill is to prevent your Service Dog from being an obstruction, to facilitate or ease travel (such as on a bus, plane or train) and to help your canine assistant be unobtrusive while in public. One of the biggest compliments a Service Dog handler or trainer can receive is, "I didn't even know a dog was there!"

To begin teaching "under," it's helpful to utilize a low table, like a coffee or end table. Lure your Service Dog in Training or Service Dog candidate under the table, from one side to the other, and tell them to down. "Down" should be built into your partner's under, and your partner should remain "under" until she's released, just like a stay.

Public Access Skills: Leave It

"Leave it" means "disregard entirely and do not engage in any way, shape, form or fashion." It's vital not only for your partner's safety, but also for basic public access manners. "Leave it" can be used to discourage inappropriate sniffing, being overly social with another person or dog, picking up food off the floor, or engaging with distractions. It's important that "leave it" be properly practiced and reinforced with a plethora of distractions before trying to use the command in new places, as dogs don't generalize behaviors or concepts well.

There are many methods of teaching leave it, but one way to begin involves offering your dog praise and a treat for redirecting from a distraction to you. When you notice your Service Dog or Service Dog in Training starting to automatically offer eye contact when faced with a distraction, you can add a verbal cue.

Public Access Skills: Heeling or Loose Leash Walking

Regardless of what you call it, the ability for your Service Dog in Training or Service Dog to be in public without dragging you, straining at the leash, coughing, choking, trying to get to distractions, etc is vital. No dog is perfect, and like any skill, loose leash walking is perfected via practice. This part of the public access skills actually involves many pieces: ignoring distractions, being focused on the handler, impulse control, being responsive to direction

Introduce public access skills in small doses, and always reinforce handler focus, changes, etc. Service Dogs need to be able to walk for several minutes at a time, focused on their handler or trainer, able to ignore distractions, before starting work in public. Note: that doesn't mean they are perfect. That means they have the basic skills necessary to redirect to the handler in the face of distraction, even if it requires verbal cueing, luring with a treat, an assistive training device or other method of securing your partner's attention and focus, like backing away from the distraction until your partner is again able to focus on you and move with you. The point of this public access skill is that you shouldn't have to fight your partner for attention. Before working in public, you and your SDiT/Service Dog need to have already figured out how to proof distractions, redirect focus and reward sustained focus.

With time, this focus exercise turns into effortless loose leash walking, but everyone starts somewhere.

Public Access Skills: House Training

This public access skill is non-negotiable. Your Service Dog must be house trained, and your Service Dog in Training, if young, must be housebroken to a schedule with regular opportunities to go outside so good habits are built.

Your partner needs to be accident free and offer a clear indication that you, the handler or trainer, can read, when they need to go outside.

House training is one of the few directly stated points in federal Service Dog law that can allow a business to remove your Service Dog from the premises, so make sure your partner is ready for an outing before beginning it.

Public Access Skills: Final Considerations

Many people will ask, "How can I prepare my dog for public access without working them in public?" What's important to realize is that your partner needs basic obedience skills before working in public, so that you guys can focus on the public-specific behaviors, manners and training without worrying about basic manners and skills. The skills above (heeling, down stays, etc) form the foundation of public access training, and they can be practiced at home and polished so that when you get in public, you already have the competence and confidence to not have to worry about fighting over food, basic distractions or stays.

Do they need to be perfect? No. Even very young puppies can go on short, 10-15 minute outings where they work one age-specific exercises, i.e. remaining sitting with the handler when someone walks by. It's all about proper foundation and reinforcing, but it's best to figure out the basics out of the public eye.[3]

Professionally Trained

To get a dog that is already trained, you should go to an agency or a private trainer. Throughout the United States and Canada are many organizations and agencies that will help you get a service dog. Each of them follows its own training procedures, and there is almost always a waiting list for a well-trained service dog.

Most puppies begin their training when they are ten to fourteen weeks old. They complete socialization and obedience training first and then learn service-dog skills.

If you are considering acquiring a service dog through an agency or organization, bear these points in mind:

➤ How quickly do you need the dog? Some agencies can provide a dog within a few months, while others have waiting lists of two to five years.

➤ How much can you afford to pay? Some agencies provide trained service dogs for free; some charge on a sliding scale; some offer financial assistance or will help you raise the money depending on your income.

➤ What level of training do you require in a service dog? People's needs vary. If you are in a wheelchair or require a dog to open doors, pick up items off the floor, or do the laundry, the training will be more extensive. If you need a dog only to alert you

---

[3] Kea Grace, "5 Public Access Skills Every Service Dog Should Know," *Anything Pawsable*, April 27, 2015, accessed June 19, 2015, http://www.anythingpawsable.com/vital-public-access-skills/#.VYS-lPm6frc

to sounds or medical conditions, that would involve a much shorter training period.

If you want to consider training by an individual professional trainer, you will need to do your homework. Be sure that you check references and visit some of the trainer's clients. Verify that the trainer understands what your needs are and knows how to train the dog accordingly. Carefully read any contracts that you may be asked to sign—you want to know exactly what tasks the trainer is going to teach the dog, the length of the training period, and what written guarantees you will receive.

A good professional trainer will follow through with maintenance, making sure that the dog's skills remain fine tuned. During a recent month-long bout of illness, Wayne asked Stacey Larsen, who owns Puppy Prep School in Scottsdale, Arizona, to give him a hand. Wayne has worked with and trained dogs since 1983, and he knew that maintenance should be kept up, even though he was too ill to do it himself. So he asked Stacey for help. Never hesitate to ask for help with your dog if you need it.

To find an individual trainer we recommend that you visit The Association of Professional Dog Trainers website at www.apdt.com.

You may also be able to locate a trainer through your local PetSmart store. Check out every organization or agency that specializes in your type of disability.

Be patient in this process. Getting a service dog is a very important part of your life—your dog will be your companion, partner, and helper twenty-four hours a day for many years. You want to take the time to make the best possible choice.

Is the Cost of Training a Service Dog Tax Deductible?

As with the costs for any medical device that you purchase, your service-dog expenses are tax deductible. You may deduct as medical expenses the costs of buying and training your service dog. You may also deduct the costs for maintaining the dog's health and vitality, such as food, grooming, veterinary care, and medications.

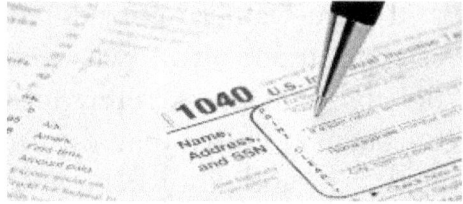

Internal Revenue Service *Publication 502* states: "You can include in medical expenses the costs of buying, training, and maintaining a guide dog or other service animal to assist a visually impaired or hearing disabled person, or a person with other physical disabilities. In general, this includes any costs, such as food, grooming, and veterinary care, incurred in maintaining the health and vitality of the service animal so that it may perform its duties."[4]

Generally, if you itemize your deductions on Schedule A, Form 1040, you may deduct only the amount of your total medical and dental expenses that exceeds ten percent of your adjusted gross income (AGI). If you or your spouse is age sixty-five or older, you may deduct only the amount that exceeds seven and one-half percent of your AGI.

For example, if your AGI is $30,000, ten percent of that amount would be $3,000. If your total medical expenses are $4,000, you must subtract $3,000—which equals ten percent of your AGI. You may then deduct the remaining $1,000.

---

[4] Internal Revenue Service *Publication 502, Medical and Dental Expenses*, http://www.irs.gov/uac/About-Publication-502, accessed June 25, 2015.

If either you or your spouse is age sixty-five or older and your AGI is $30,000, seven and one-half percent of that amount would be $2,250. If your total medical expenses are $4,000, you must subtract $2,250—which equals seven and one-half percent of your AGI. You may then deduct the remaining $1,750.

If you are ever audited by the IRS you may be asked to provide proof that your dog qualifies as a service animal under ADA guidelines. We recommend that, if you train your own service dog, you keep a record of the training either in a notebook, on video tape, or in an online weblog. And, of course, keep and catalog all receipts for expenses related to your service dog.

We are not accountants or financial advisors and we do not intend to give accounting or other professional advice. If you have questions, we suggest that you consult with a tax professional.

Discretionary Disobedience

There are times when the dog knows better than you do— what a surprise! You may be encouraging the dog to move forward or to stay in place when he knows there is danger that you haven't detected. He is smart enough to get your attention and disobey you for your protection—so learn to always *listen to your dog*.

If Wayne ignores Shadow's communication or puts him off, Shadow stands on his hind legs and nudges Wayne on his chest or back to make him pay attention.

As you let your dog know that you expect him to alert you about what you need, he will start doing more and more to help you.

Remember that training must be reinforced constantly, even after the dog is perfectly trained. Don't forget—he is still a dog.

Family Relationships

Family dynamics play an important part in having a service dog in your home. We believe that a loving family life—with or without other animals—is a healthy environment for your service dog. Your dog will bond with you because you are the one who feeds him, grooms him, and takes care of him—and because you are the person who requires him to be close by and aware of you.

Your dog will also be aware of other disabled or sick people in your family and may alert on their issues.

Sometimes healthy family members may become jealous because of the attention that the disabled person receives from his/her dog. This has to be overcome.

While our dog works for Wayne solely, Anne has diabetes and so the dog naturally alerts on her body odors to let her know when her blood sugar is too low and she needs to eat. One day she fell, and during the next week, as she rested and recuperated, the dog lay next to her to comfort and help her.

A Happy, Well-Adjusted Service Dog

It is important for your dog to be well adjusted. Shadow has play dates and sleepovers with his friends. He is very sociable, as he should be when he is "off the clock." Being a service dog does not mean he is in servitude—it means

Shadow in his fancy dress!

he has a job and responsibilities. Dogs *love* to have a job. But when you take a break, so does your dog.

Our dog works daily. We lead a very active life, and he goes everywhere with us: to trade shows and conventions, to political meetings, and to social functions. He needs regular relaxation, just as any person would.

Your dog will quickly learn that, when wearing his vest, he is on the job and working; and, when the vest comes off, he is free to relax. When our dog is wearing the vest he is not "allowed" to be social—he is working, and he understands that. When we take his vest off, he is allowed to "say hello."

Shadow is friendly and has very good manners. He always acknowledges our friends and other service dogs when we meet, and then he lies down. If we take off his vest, he gets to

Snow Prince enjoying a limo ride on the way to a gala

schmooze with them. However, sometimes he just does whatever he wants to do in his "free time!"

75

You can tell from the photo of Shadow in his fancy formal dress that it is hard for him to be "neutral." We think he likes getting his white hair on people's black tuxes!

Just as you depend on your dog for protection, he also relies on you to protect him. For a dog, going out into the public arena with strange sights, sounds, and smells is very stressful. When we return home from a long trip or convention Shadow, like Snow Prince before him, goes into his version of seclusion for about a week to chill out—just like we do!

When you are at home, your dog will still be "working" but may not be as tightly focused because he knows you are in a safe environment.

"A dog can't think that much about what he's doing, he just does what feels right."
—Barbara Kingsolver

PART IV

Health and Wellness

Grooming

Grooming is one of the most important methods of bonding with your dog. If you are raising your own puppy, you usually get your puppy when he is between ten and fourteen weeks old. To groom, you first pet your puppy; this expresses affection and lets

him get used to your touching him all over. This is an important part of grooming—don't skip it.

Always make sure to clean between your dog's toes. Your dog must get used to your handling his toes and feet, not only for grooming but also because you will be putting on and taking off his boots or shoes (this will be explained later in this chapter).

Wayne uses two grooming tools: the standard comb, which detangles the dog's hair and under coat, and the shedding blade, which takes care of the outer coat. Wayne grooms Shadow at least once a day and, if we are attending an evening event, again just before we leave for the event.

We recommend choosing a breed with grooming needs that suit your lifestyle, abilities, and pocketbook. Our beautiful White German Shepherd could fill a small mattress every time we bathe him—he blows his coat twice a year and sheds the rest of the time. A Chihuahua does neither, but Wayne is 6 feet 5 inches tall and would look really silly walking a Chihuahua! Most long-haired dogs require bathing at least once or twice a month; their bodies emit oil much like the hair on our heads does. Poodles must be taken to a groomer—expensive, if that is a concern.

Wayne prefers to groom his dog himself. Fortunately, we have a walk-in shower, so Wayne can use a shower wand to wash the dog. Wayne bathes Shadow every two to three weeks. During allergy season, because Wayne has allergies, he takes the dog into the shower and rinses off his coat daily with water to remove dander and dust.

We have witnessed improperly trained groomers mishandling dogs. When traveling for long periods of time we carry grooming gear with us—a shedding blade, toenail clippers, and a Kong grooming brush to get Shadow's thick undercoat off during bathing.

It's time consuming to bathe a White German Shepherd, and we are lucky that Shadow can go into the shower with Wayne and then get blow dried (did you ever?!). It's different with smaller dogs. Poodles and other breeds require a groomer. But whatever method you use, you must be sure that your dog is clean both for health reasons and for odors and critters that may attach. Dogs have a body smell much like humans do—imagine not bathing for a month! They sweat in the summer and emit an odor when nervous. Their coats get matted when their oil glands secrete. For a host of reasons, it's important to keep them clean and well groomed.

If you are grooming your dog yourself, use a good-quality shampoo that contains moisturizers. Be sure to get all the soap out of the dog's coat so that he doesn't itch.

Cold-Weather Care

Many dogs need boots or shoes in cold weather as well as hot weather, regardless of coat length. If your dog frequently lifts his paws, whines, or stops during walks, his feet are uncomfortably cold or hot. Be sure to get your dog used to wearing shoes before very hot or very

cold weather sets in. The formation of ice balls between the pads and toes of a dog's feet is a common problem. This is painful—like walking on rocks! When ice balls have formed, dogs often whine, stop walking, and start chewing at the bottoms of their feet. To help prevent this, trim the hair around your dog's feet. If your dog walks on salted sidewalks or streets be sure to wash his paws after this exposure. Salt is irritating to your dog's footpads.

Ear tips are especially susceptible to frostbite, so take precautions.

Keep your dog away from antifreeze solution, and promptly clean up any antifreeze that spills. Antifreeze is attractive and tastes sweet to dogs, but it is deadly, even in minute amounts. Poinsettias are festive decorations at holiday time, but they are very poisonous to dogs, so keep them well away from your dog.

Dogs with very short coats have the lowest tolerance for cold. Extremely short-coated breeds include Greyhounds, Dobermans, Boxers, Boston Terriers, and Chihuahuas. These breeds should not go outside in cold weather without their sweaters or jackets except for short times to relieve themselves. Small dogs with short coats may not be able to tolerate any outdoor exercise or work in extremely cold weather. Your dog should wear his service vest in all weather conditions and, if it is raining, a raincoat.

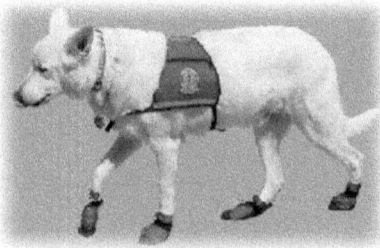

Snow Prince sporting his new shoes. He wouldn't get out of the car without them.

Hot-Weather Care

Dogs were never meant to walk on concrete or asphalt. Our working dogs suffer when their pads burn. If you can't comfortably place your hand on the pavement, it is time to put shoes on your dog. He *will* get used to them. Let him wear the shoes in the house for a few minutes at a time, then for an hour, then for a couple of hours. Eventually, he will appreciate his shoes.

Remember that dogs breathe through their paws! Avoid shoes that do not breathe or let your dog's paws breathe. Hard-molded rubber soles should be reserved for search-and-rescue work or for walking on sharp or dangerous material for short periods.

Diet

Your dog deserves to be fed well. How and when you feed him is determined by his breed and size as well as your schedule. Ask your vet to recommend the best type of food and a meal schedule. There is no one best way, but whichever way you choose—stay with it. Dogs have tender digestive systems, and it is no fun to be out and about with a dog that's throwing up or pooping everywhere.

Changing a dog's diet is no simple task. Once you find what he likes and what suits him, stick with it if possible. If changes need to be made, they should be made gradually when you are ready and have the time to deal with the results.

We vary Shadow's diet within a family of food products. He gets lamb, rice, salmon, and duck—frankly, he eats better than we do! This gives his coat a nice shine, too.

Controlling what your dog eats is important. If you are an active person, you will be going to coffee shops, restaurants, cafeterias, etc. Your dog should not beg for food from tables or eat things that upset his stomach. The dog should learn to eat only out of his dog bowl or one of his foldable pet dishes. Shadow knows that he will never get food that is not in his proper bowl, that whatever is in his bowl is safe to eat, and that he is allowed to eat it.

Another reason to train your dog to eat this way is that it may prevent someone from using food to entice and steal him. Service dogs are valuable and much desired because of their temperament and training. It is not uncommon for people to try to steal them.

Wayne's dog gets special treats only from Anne or from a designated couple who take care of him in emergencies. Your dog should learn to accept food only if it is in his bowl or travel container and to accept treats only from designated people.

It is easy to train your service dog to not sniff food on the table or grab morsels off the table to eat. How? From the moment your dog comes to you, *never* feed him any way other than as described above. If you follow this simple rule, you will be able to dine in restaurants or attend any function without having to worry about your dog's sniffing, touching, or tasting food in his vicinity.

Feed your dog whatever type of food your veterinarian recommends. Wayne only feeds Shadow food that is made in the United States. He occasionally adds a teaspoon of vegetable oil to keep Shadow's skin moisturized. Wayne does not feed his dog any table scraps. And, although many people favor the BARF diet (which includes bones and raw food), we do not use it. Because we travel often, we want Shadow to eat only dog food that we can purchase along the way and carry with us. We don't recommend changing your dog's diet while away from home because it could upset his stomach. Many brands are available in travel pouches.

Dental Care

Let's talk teeth! Having your dog's teeth cleaned can be pricey. There are many options available, and you can brush your dog's teeth at home in several different ways. Talk with your veterinarian or visit your pet-supply store to choose.

Although there are treats that will help clean plaque and tartar off your dog's teeth, you cannot replace professional cleaning. You should choose a veterinarian whose medical plan for your dog includes teeth cleaning.

To brush Shadow's teeth, Wayne uses a device similar to a little rubber bush that fits over his index finger.

Medical Care

It is vital for your dog to receive regular vaccinations (just as *you* get a flu shot each year). And the law requires that your dog be up to date on shots when entering certain public places or traveling.

Some veterinarians offer economical wellness plans that allow you to go into the office at the first sign of any medical need. Insurance plans are also available; you can find information about these from your vet or through an internet search.

We prefer Banfield Pet Hospital, housed in PetSmart stores, because we travel a great deal. We can go into any PetSmart in the U.S. and receive treatment for Shadow at a reasonable price; and they have our dog's records on file electronically.

Banfield offers several levels of plans; ours costs approximately $35 per month. It includes walk-in visits at no charge, medication discounts, many vaccinations at no cost, and quite a few other perks.

A number of insurance plans are available. Look into several and determine which suits you.

A CareCredit card or similar dedicated health-care card will allow you to conveniently charge the dog's medical-care costs and your own, if you wish. We have used our CareCredit card both for our dog's medical expenses ($2,500 tumor removal) and for Anne's.

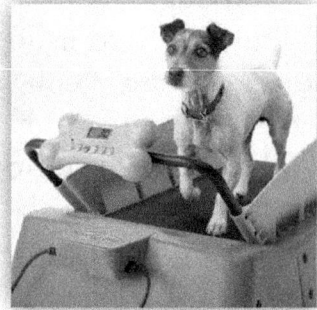

Giving your dog medication is easy if, from the beginning, you give it without food by gently putting it down his throat. Sometimes, if a pill is large, Wayne breaks it in half and gives it to Shadow in food.

Exercise

You know it—we *ALL* need exercise! Both your dog and you will benefit from his need to get out and mix it up with the other dogs. There are many choices—walking, jogging, the dog park, hiking, swimming (in your own pool, please), playing Frisbee, bicycling with your dog running alongside you.

Our Snow Prince wouldn't touch water and Shadow only likes to get his feet wet—but Labs love water.

If you are walking your dog mostly for his benefit, be sure to allow him time to sniff. This is how he gets his information—it takes time to find just the right place to "go" or to find a playmate. Sniffing another dog's rear end is good etiquette among dogs and should be allowed.

Take time to be sure that you aren't dragging your dog because you are in a hurry and have longer legs.

Wayne likes using his TRX Personal Transporter to exercise his dog.

Etiquette

When you're out and about with your service dog, be mindful of others. Remember that some people are allergic to dogs or afraid of dogs, and you may be asked to accommodate their needs. Please make this allowance as others make allowances for you—without taking offense.

> An assistance dog should not interfere or inconvenience the public in any way. There are people who don't like dogs, are afraid of dogs or allergic to dogs. Many people have never seen a dog working in public and are quite startled when they sit down in a restaurant and see a dog lying under the table, or standing next to them in a small elevator. It's very important to leave a good impression with the public. We want to

insure the rights of all people with disabilities to continue to work with assistance dogs in public access situations.

An assistance dog should:

* Lie quietly while the handler is dining without grooming itself or scratching.
* Be allowed to toilet only in areas where people do not sit or walk, and the handler should have a method for cleaning up and disposing of droppings immediately.
* Move purposefully next to its handler while working, staying between 12-18 inches from the handler's side unless it has been cued to perform another task.
* Work comfortably and reliably, giving its handler focus when necessary.

An assistance dog should *NOT*:

* Be allowed to wander in public.
* Initiate social contact without its handler's permission.
* Sniff, beg, or eat from the floor in a restaurant or public setting.
* Bite, snap, bark, whine, or growl, causing a disruption or danger to the public.
* Block the areas where the public will be walking.
* Press against, jump on or sniff people.

Working in public access situations with a specially trained assistance dog is a privilege and a joy. A combination of the right dog with proper training of both dog and human partners will create a successful working team.[5]

DO NOT POOP and LEAVE!

No one wants to step in your dog's stuff! It takes only a few seconds to take a plastic bag, turn it inside out, scoop up your dog's poop, pull the bag back over your hand, and tie a knot in it.

You will *NEVER* be welcome anywhere if you are not a considerate dog owner. Your dog should never be allowed to relieve himself on a sidewalk or in a hallway or elevator. Good manners are good manners—no matter where you are and no matter if you are human or animal.

When your dog needs to relieve himself, try to find a place that is private and out of the way. Take off his vest as a signal that it's time to "go." If people approach you to pet the dog or "talk" to him while he is relieving himself, this is distracting and the dog will probably not be able to complete his task. This makes him uncomfortable, which puts him in a bad mood, and then he can't concentrate on his job. Be sure people understand that he needs some space. They wouldn't like having a parade in their bathroom!

Socialization

It is extremely important that your dog interact comfortably with people and with other dogs. If he is inappropriately sniffing, growling, or

---

[5] Shari Dehouwer, "Training an Assistance Dog for Public Access," in *The Golden Bridge*, ed. Patty Dobbs Gross (West Lafayette IN: Purdue University Press, 2005), 199-204.

barking while wearing his working vest, you will NOT be welcome. And your dog will not appear to be well trained. If necessary, get a trainer to help.

The more places you take your dog, the better he will understand his job and how to behave appropriately in public. Start with small crowds and then enlarge his experience. If he isn't used to children, the shopping mall is a great place to train; it's also a handy place to teach your dog how to use elevators, escalators, and stairs. Our dog has play dates at the dog park every day. Your dog needs to socialize and, if you give him plenty of opportunities, he will quickly learn.

"His ears were often the first thing to catch my tears."
—Elizabeth Barrett Browning referring to her cocker spaniel, Flush

PART V

Travel with Your Service Dog

Wayne never goes on any trip without the dog's travel bag. Since Wayne and Shadow are on the road a lot, the dog needs many different items during a trip.

Shadow travels with his own luggage including a carry-on wheeled backpack. Some of the items that we carry are:

- ✓ Service-dog clothing and identification
- ✓ Mesh muzzle
- ✓ Blanket (the type you put on the couch or car seat—can be purchased at Costco or any pet store)
- ✓ Roll of paper towels for emergencies
- ✓ Food dish and water bowl

✓ Package/can of food, can opener, fork for stirring, plastic can cover if necessary
✓ Lint brush
✓ Medication
✓ First-aid kit
✓ Two-inch flashlight
✓ Poop bags
✓ Flashing/blinking dog collar/leash for night walking
✓ Sixteen-foot extendable leash for walking and exercise
✓ Brush or shedding blade for grooming
✓ Raincoat/shoes

Remember to check weather forecasts for your destination and pack accordingly for your service dog.

A MUST DO!! If you're traveling outside your normal locale, protect your dog with flea and tick medicine or collar before you leave—particularly if you will be traveling in wooded areas, humid areas, or other areas where fleas and ticks are prevalent.

By Car

We suggest that, when you travel by car, your dog wear his service-dog vest. You are not legally required to have your dog in a vest, but people expect to see one and it does make public access easier.

We also recommend that you carry service-dog ID and your ADA card. Again, these are not required, but if you are confronted by someone who objects to your dog's being in a public place, the federal-law card and service-dog ID usually do the trick.

You do NOT have to pay a surcharge or a pet deposit for a service dog at a hotel, but hotel staff will be less likely to question you if your dog is wearing his work outfit and you have ID at hand.

Keep a bed in the back of the car for your dog's comfort, and don't forget to make frequent stops so your dog can stretch his legs, drink water, and take relief breaks. *PLEASE* do not let your dog hang his head out the window—road debris or insects might get into his eyes and hurt him.

By Air

Traveling on an airplane together for the first time can be very stressful for a service-dog team. We offer these suggestions to help you until you and your dog have become experienced travelers.

Airlines usually have a weight restriction of eighty-five pounds for dogs. If you have a small dog, you may use a carrier, which you slide under the seat until after takeoff. If you have a nervous dog, your veterinarian can provide an anxiety medication or you may use Rescue Remedy—a natural stress reliever that is available at health-food stores.

When we travel, we make our reservations online (it is often less expensive) and then follow up immediately with a telephone call to the airline to indicate that we will be traveling with a service dog. We reserve bulkhead seats.

The dog lies at our feet on his blanket in the bulkhead area. The blanket has Shadow's scent on it; this calms him. It rolls up and fits into the backpack. We lay it on the floor so that:

- Our dog has a comfortable place to lie—the floor can get hard and hot
- There will be less dog hair on the cabin floor (always appreciated by airline staff)

As soon as we get into the cabin, we lay the blanket down and Shadow backs into the space so that his head faces the aisle. All dogs want to be able to see and hear what is going on, but this is especially true of a service dog, whose job is to be aware of his surroundings and alert his partner to what is happening. If you don't back your dog into the position that we suggest, then your dog will keep getting up, turning around, or standing so that he can see and hear what is going on. It's his job to alert you, so he will find a way to remain aware.

When Shadow alerts, he touches Wayne, looks toward where the activity that Wayne needs to notice is occurring, and waits for Wayne to acknowledge the alert. If Wayne doesn't pay attention to the alert, Shadow goes to his next alert signal, which is to paw Wayne's leg. The dog's alerts increase in intensity if his partner doesn't acknowledge the signals. Being unable to see or hear what is happening and alert Wayne, if needed, would make Shadow very anxious.

Always ask to preboard. That allows you time to get your dog settled before the main boarding begins.

After we have boarded and gotten settled, Shadow lies down and goes to sleep. We remove his vest while we're on the plane so that he is more comfortable.

You could hold a small dog in your lap, but you may not want to do this for the duration of the flight. Settling the dog on the floor, as we do with Shadow, gives you more freedom in your seat.

Our dog is over the weight limit, but we find that, when airline personnel see that Wayne cannot walk unless Shadow is with him to stabilize him, they don't object.

Even though the airline may have a weight limit, federal law for service dogs does not and the Department of Justice will take your part in a dispute with an airline.

Sometimes we're not able to get seats in the bulkhead, and sometimes we sit with our feet against the wall because someone has been seated in the third seat. But most of the time we can travel comfortably. In any event, the airline *MUST* allow your service dog to be in the cabin with you. There is no surcharge for your service dog.

It is best to not feed your dog after 6 p.m. the night before airline travel, and any water that he gets after awakening in the morning should be used to wet his lips—not to drink. On the way to the airport you should take him to the dog park to run, make sure he relieves himself, and take him to relieve himself again at the airport before you go through security. By law, airports must provide service-dog relief areas, though most are outside the security areas. Some airports have installed relief areas inside the security gates, so do ask.

You will be required to have a health certificate for your dog, issued within ten days before travel from the city in which your flight originates. Your veterinarian can provide the certificate.

Before flying internationally, you must find out the requirements for entering each country that you will visit. You will need an international health certificate, which your veterinarian can provide.

Www.PetTravel.com offers information, forms, and documents that you will need for travel outside the U.S.

By Sea

When booking your travel, tell the cruise line that a service dog travels with you, and you will be advised what that cruise line's policies are.

Cruise lines usually require an international health certificate. You must complete an Animal and Plant Health Inspection Service (APHIS) form, which your veterinarian will have, and send a copy to the cruise line. Information on the APHIS form is available at the following website: www.aphis.usda.gov/animal_health.

94

The cruise line will provide a relief area on the ship. The size of these will vary, so be prepared! After you have settled into your cabin, the purser's office can tell you where the relief area is located.

One cruise line provided a 30-inch by 30-inch acrylic box filled with some type of doggie litter. Since our Snow Prince was a big boy, this was quite a challenge! It actually took thirty-six hours before he would relieve himself the first time—but he finally did, with no bad after-effects.

If your cabin has a balcony, your dog's relief area might be located there. On one ship the relief area was located in a crew walkway across from our cabin. It was once on another deck of the ship!

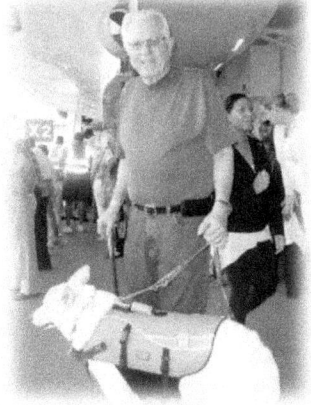

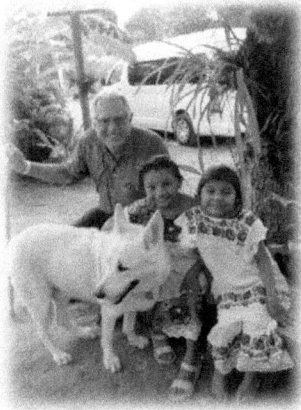

Taking your service dog into the ship's food court or dining room is not a problem. The maître d' will always find a table for you that is large enough and out of the path of foot traffic. Corner tables are sometimes best. You want your dog to be comfortable and at ease, not fearful that he will be stepped on! We also make sure that we have a foldable water dish with us and give our dog water during our meal or snack.

We take a life vest for our dog, and we glue his service-dog patch to it. We have never experienced any problems while traveling onboard cruise ships with our service dog and have always felt very welcome aboard the ships.

Remember that you must carry onboard whatever food you plan to feed your service dog, whatever vitamins or medications he will need, and his favorite toys!

The more you walk on the ship, the more exercise your dog will get. Most ships have an upper deck with a jogging track or fenced-in basketball court. Larger dogs in particular will feel joint stiffness if they can't exercise regularly, so be sure to walk your dog while onboard.

There may be ports of call where your dog is not allowed to leave the ship. For example, your dog will not be allowed to disembark at any country/island under British rule due to quarantine laws. In Barbados, we had to leave our dog onboard for five hours—just like when he stays at home. *Bon voyage!*

It is your responsibility to know what the regulations are in the ports that you will visit; your veterinarian or the cruise line will have this information.

By Train

As with other travel, be sure to get in touch with the train company to find out its policies.

We have traveled on only a couple of trains for short trips. We carried the dog's travel bag and made sure that he relieved himself before we got on the train. As soon as we got off the train we gave him a relief break.

If you take your service dog with you in a commute to work by subway or train, we suggest carrying a small dog-travel bag, since sooner or later you will need some of the

items in a travel bag. Always carry water, a foldable water dish, and poop bags.

Hotel Accommodations

Hotel accommodations are not usually a problem for people traveling with service dogs; however, occasionally they can be! When we sign in at a hotel, we always tell the desk clerk that we have a service dog with us; that the dog is wearing his vest, his service-dog collar, and a leash; and that we have his ID card and the ADA card regarding service dogs.

Remember that the hotel most likely has a "no pet" policy. Putting your dog's work outfit on lets everyone know that your dog is not a pet but a working dog.

By carrying a copy of the ADA card, you can educate hotel staff who may not be aware of federal law regarding service dogs. Remember that, if your dog is denied lodging at a hotel, you have recourse through the U.S. Department of Justice or the state attorney general.

While staying at a hotel, always carry poop bags in your pocket or purse. We guarantee that you will not notice all the people who are watching you and your dog. So make sure that you always pick up your dog's droppings. There is usually a trash container near the hotel entrance where you can deposit the waste.

Before making reservations, we visit hotel websites and look at photos of the grounds to make sure there is a place to walk our service dog—a grassy area or walking path. Many hotels, especially in large cities, directly front the sidewalk and have no lawn areas. On more than one occasion, Wayne has had to walk several blocks to find grass. This is no fun, especially late at night or in bad weather. This may not be a problem if your dog is trained for city living.

We once stayed overnight with friends at their timeshare. The management was informed that our service dog would be staying. There were other dogs on the premises that were not service dogs. Our friends were charged $250 for the night! When we learned this, we immediately filed a complaint with the attorney general of the state we were in—our friends received a refund of the $250

"I believe in integrity. Dogs have it. Humans are sometimes lacking it."
—Cesar Millan

A Final Word

You now have the ins and outs, the truths and myths of service-dog handling. We hope that this book has given you a better understanding of the special bond and incredible experience of partnering with a service dog.

Mostly you need to exercise common sense and listen to your dog. And remember that, as your physical needs change, so will your dog's behavior change to suit your new circumstances.

So go and enjoy this extraordinary relationship!

Appendix A
Recommended Resources

Here are a few of the places that can help you:

State Attorney General	Your state website
State Commission for Deaf and Hard of Hearing	Your state (there is one in every state)
Delta Society	www.deltasociety.org
Assn. for Late Deafened Adults	www.alda.org
Hearing Loss Assn. of America	www.hearingloss.org
Intl. Assn. of Assistance Dog Partners	www.iaadp.org
Deaf Hire	www.deafhire.com
National listing of interest groups	www.meetups.com
U.S. Department of Agriculture	www.aphis.usda.gov
U.S. Department of Justice	www.usdoj.gov

We recommend these books and videos:

TOP DOG (www.topdogusa.org)

My Ears Have a Wet Nose: Acquiring, Training and Loving a Hearing Dog
by Anne Wicklund

Working Like Dogs: The Service Dog Guidebook
by Marcie Davis and Melissa Bunnell

Support groups:

International Association of Assistance Dog Partners (IAADP)
Assistance Dogs International (ADI)
Pet Partners (formerly Delta Society)

Appendix B
Federal Law Regarding Service Animals

The federal civil rights law, the Americans with Disabilities Act of 1990, Title III, 28 Code of Federal Regulations, s. 36.104, defines a service dog as:

> any dog that is individually trained to do work or perform tasks for the benefit of an individual with a disability, including a physical, sensory, psychiatric, intellectual, or other mental disability. Other species of animals, whether wild or domestic, trained or untrained, are not service animals for the purposes of this definition. The work or tasks performed by a service animal must be directly related to the individual's disability. Examples of work or tasks include, but are not limited to, assisting individuals who are blind or have low vision with navigation and other tasks, alerting individuals who are deaf or hard of hearing to the presence of people or sounds, providing nonviolent protection or rescue work, pulling a wheelchair, assisting an individual during a seizure, alerting individuals to the presence of allergens, retrieving items such as medicine or the telephone, providing physical support and assistance with balance and stability to individuals with mobility disabilities, and helping persons with psychiatric and neurological disabilities by preventing or interrupting impulsive or destructive behaviors.

By law, a service dog is not considered a pet and is therefore not subject to pet restrictions. It is prohibited by law to require proof or "certification" of a service dog's training.

ADA regulations have been revised to designate miniature horses that have been individually trained to perform tasks for disabled people as service animals. A disabled individual must be allowed to bring a miniature horse onto the premises of public places or private businesses as long as the horse has been individually trained to do work or perform tasks for the benefit of that individual and as long as the facility can accommodate the miniature horse's type, size, and weight. The rules that apply to service dogs also apply to miniature horses.

Federal (e.g., ADA 28 CFR, s. 38.302) and state laws protect the right of disabled individuals to be accompanied by their trained service animals in taxis, buses, trains, stores, restaurants, doctors' offices, schools, parks, housing, and other public places.

In addition to the ADA, federal laws that protect individuals with disabilities include: the Fair Housing Amendments Act (1988); s. 504 of the Rehabilitation Act (1973); the Air Carrier Access Act (1986); and other regulations.

If federal and state or local laws conflict, the law that is less restrictive for the disabled individual prevails. For example, if state law grants access only to service dogs that do guide work, and the service dog in question performs work other than guide work, federal law will apply. The disabled individual must be permitted access with the service dog.

A person who is accompanied by a service dog is legally responsible for its stewardship (behavior, care, and well being), must obey animal-welfare laws (such as leash, cruelty, or other similar regulations), and is liable for any damage done by the service animal.

For further information about the ADA, contact the U.S. Department of Justice ADA Information Line at 800-514-0301 (V) or 800-514-0383 (TDD.) For your state's information, contact your attorney general.

Index

G

About the Authors

In 2000 Anne and Wayne Wicklund bought a White German Shepherd named Snow Prince. Coincidentally Wayne found that he was losing his hearing. His frustration grew as he was unable to find ways to let other people know that he could not hear, so Wayne and Anne started a company called hearingimpaired.net, Inc. to develop communication aids for hearing-impaired people.

Snow Prince began to exhibit strange behaviors, and Anne

and Wayne eventually realized that he was trying to warn Wayne about dangerous or noisy things. Wayne, who had studied at the Rudy Drexler School for Dogs and had become a Master Trainer, now began to train Snow Prince to become a hearing-assist dog.

Unable to find accessories to identify Snow Prince as a working service dog, Wayne and Anne started to produce their own devices and now provide service-dog supplies (vests, patches, ID cards, etc.) as well as much-needed information through

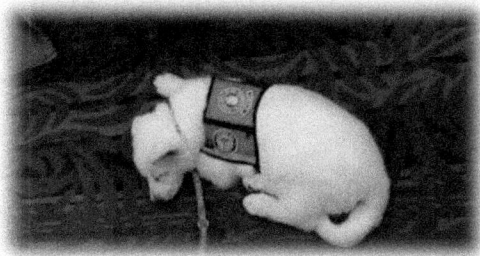

their businesses, hearingimpaired.net, Inc. and MrPAWS by Snow.

In 2006 Wayne became very ill and Snow Prince began to work with Wayne's medical issues as well. In 2013 Snow Prince passed away. His successor, Snow Shadow, now takes care of Wayne and is doing an admirable job at a very young age.

Anne has published two previous books: *My Ears Have a Wet Nose: Acquiring, Loving and Training a Hearing Dog* and an educational coloring book about service dogs titled *I Have a Wet Nose . . . and I Have a Job.*

The Wicklunds are active politically in order to help lawmakers make good decisions about service-dog handlers' rights, and they work with several lawmakers and agencies including the Veterans Administration and its service-dog program. They also work with airport managers, advocating for service-dog relief areas.

Wayne, Anne, and Snow Shadow live in Fountain Hills, Arizona.

Anne and Wayne Wicklund are the owners of hearingimpaired.net, Inc. and MrPAWS by Snow. They are a great resource for all things about service dogs. Wayne's health issues led to the creation of many products that you will not find elsewhere. To learn more about the range of products available or to suggest new ones, contact Anne and Wayne at: www.mrpaws.com or
www.hearingimpaired.net.

Professional Memberships:
HLAA (Hearing Loss Association of America)
ALDA (Association for Late Deafened Adults)
IAADP (International Association of Assistance Dog Partners)
ADI (Assistance Dogs International)
CAzAD (Connecting Arizona Advocates), Board Member
Arizona Disability Advocacy Coalition, Board Member
PAD (Phoenix Association for the Deaf)
AAD (Arizona Association for the Deaf)

Contact information:
Anne and Wayne Wicklund
P O Box 17954
Fountain Hills, AZ 85269
(480) 837-0190
anne@annewicklund.com
wayne@waynewicklund.com
www.handbookforservicedogs.com

Notes

Notes

Notes

Notes

Notes

Notes

www.ingramcontent.com/pod-product-compliance
Lightning Source LLC
La Vergne TN
LVHW021513080426
835509LV00018B/2500